Psychologists

Psychologists

Personal and Theoretical Pathways

Richard W. Coan

University of Arizona

IRVINGTON PUBLISHERS, INC., NEW YORK

HALSTED PRESS Division of
JOHN WILEY & SONS, Inc.
NEW YORK   LONDON   SYDNEY   TORONTO

Distributed by Halsted Press
A division of John Wiley & Sons, Inc., New York

Library of Congress Cataloging in Publication Data

Main entry under title:

Coan, Richard W.
  Psychologists.

  1. Psychologists—Psychology. 2. Psychology—
Philosophy.   I. Title.
BF109.A1C6   150'.1   79-13711
ISBN 0-470-26785-2

Printed in the United States of America

Contents

Preface

In their professional work, psychologists usually direct their attention to other people. They rarely think of themselves as suitable objects for scientific investigation. Yet psychologists are people, and psychology—like every other science—is a form of human behavior. In this book, I shall report the results of several years of effort devoted to making sense of this form of human behavior and of the people who engage in it.

In the course of my efforts I have requested and obtained data from hundreds of psychologists. I doubt that anyone else in the history of psychology has secured nearly so much free labor from his fellow psychologists for research purposes, and I am profoundly grateful to those who have participated in this venture.

I also appreciate the many comments, both positive and negative, that I have received in the course of my work from those to whom I have sent my forms, for I have learned many unexpected things from them. I discovered early that psychologists as a group are ever-ready to evaluate the efforts of their fellows. When one is undertaking questionnaire research, it would be difficult to find a more critical population of subjects. If there are flaws in item construction and test design, these subjects are bound to spot them and call them to one's attention. Surmising the basic trend of one's investigation from one mailed form, they will send back assorted bits of methodological advice. I must confess that I have sometimes found these unsolicited responses quite helpful.

It is illuminating to me to discover the range of reactions from psychologists not only to the theoretical questions I have posed but to the research itself. I am grateful to those who have seen this as a valuable contribution to an important area of investigation. But I am also grateful to the correspondent who told me that with the world rapidly going to hell, no psychologist should waste his time playing intellectual games like this. He may well be right, of course, and there have been times when I have felt inclined to share his view. Right or wrong, he has contributed to my understanding of those curious folk who specialize in the art and science of psychology.

In undertaking a study of the biases of psychologists, I must acknowledge that I too am a psychologist and that I too have biases which incline me very strongly in a subjectivistic direction. I have entered into this research with much personal involvement and make no pretense of maintaining the kind of disinterest which—though impossible of attainment—is sometimes regarded as an ideal in science. My primary motivation with respect to this new research territory, however, is to understand it, not to demonstrate the superiority of a particular bias. There are many possible approaches to an understanding of human behavior and experience, and we need them all. There are things we can learn by studying pathways in the nervous system, by observing animals in mazes and problem boxes, by performing mathematical analyses of quantitative data, by practicing meditation, and by listening closely to our fantasies and dreams. I have little quarrel with anyone who chooses any of these routes—unless he or she insists that it is the one true path and condemns those who follow a different course. It does not particularly concern me whether some of the chosen routes deviate from the path of "true science"—a term subject to varying interpretations. If some of the things that psychologists do are poor science, many of them are also abominable poetry. If they add to our understanding of people, they may still be good psychology.

Richard W. Coan

Psychologists

1. The Psychology of Psychology

With the tremendous growth in science and the mushrooming population of scientists of recent decades, there has been a noticeable (though less dramatic) increase in activities aimed at augmenting our understanding of the nature of science. These activities constitute the general realm of metascience, or the science of science. K. B. Madsen has provided a useful logical analysis of the domain of metascience.[1] He views it as consisting of these component disciplines:

1. The philosophy of science
2. The history of science
3. The sociology of science
4. The psychology of science

The first of these would comprise three subdisciplines: epistemology, methodology, and metatheory, or systematology. The territory of the history of science is obvious. This is the one metascientific discipline that has long been part of the established subject matter of writing and teaching for scientists themselves, as well as for philosophers and historians. The sociology of science would be concerned with institutional and professional developments within the sciences and with the relationship between developments in science and the societal context in which they occur. The psychology of science would deal with such issues as the perceptual and cognitive processes of scientists, the motivation of scientific activity, and personal characteristics of scientists. From the standpoint of the psychology of science, science is a form of human activity, and it is important to seek an understanding of that activity and of the people who engage in it.

As a subdiscipline within the psychology of science, the psychology of psychology is concerned focally with psychologists and with the scientific activities of psychologists. Elsewhere I have suggested

1

that we may think of the purposes of this subdiscipline in terms of four major questions that it seeks to answer:

1. What are the psychological roots of psychology *qua* intellectual discipline? (Why do psychology and other intellectual disciplines exist?)
2. What are the roots of this particular discipline? (Why does psychology exist as a distinct discipline?)
3. Why do psychologists choose to become psychologists?
4. Why do psychologists select the theoretical and methodological positions that they do within psychology?[2]

The first question really belongs to the domain of the psychology of science in general, for it concerns the motivational foundations of all the sciences. For that matter, we can pose it with respect to a still broader domain that encompasses not only science but the arts, philosophy, religion, and mythology. To understand the roots of psychology, we must understand the motivational sources that it shares with other fields. In the second question, however, we then ask what features of human nature and the human condition prompt the existence of this particular discipline.

The third and fourth questions are closely related to the second, but they bring our attention to the characteristics of individuals who choose to become psychologists and then choose particular pathways with respect to subject matter, theory, and method once they have entered the field. Psychology is a peculiarly heterogeneous science with a far-flung and shifting boundary line. Within psychology one may pursue a career that borders on physiology, sociology, or philosophy. One may preoccupy himself with factual research data, with very abstract theoretical issues, or with the very immediate qualities and experiences of the people with whom he interacts. One may take any of a number of sharply contrasting stances with respect to the theoretical assumptions and methods that are deemed appropriate for psychologists. In most of the work that I shall report in this book I have attempted to gain a clearer picture of the nature of these choices and then to determine why psychologists make the choices that they do. I should like first, however, to consider the broader issues represented by the first two questions.

THE NATURE OF SCIENCE

Questions are raised recurrently about the relationship between science and art, philosophy, and religion. Merely to inquire about the differences among these disciplines is to grant that they have much in common, and it is really in very recent times that science has come to be viewed as something separate from philosophy. If we look for the psychological roots of science—the basic promptings in human nature and in the human condition that have led to the creation of science—we are bound to be impressed with all the characteristics that science shares with a host of other symbol-producing activities. There are many ways in which we could conceptualize the motivational source underlying science. Yet however we conceptualize it, it appears to be essentially the same human tendency that underlies art, philosophy, religion, mythology, and other systems of thought. This tendency that is common to all these varied enterprises, whether we call it a drive or an instinct or a need, is one that basically distinguishes human beings from all other species on this planet.

The basic characteristic common to science and to all the nonscientific disciplines is an effort to impose a certain order on human experience. Our experience is arranged and submitted to a structure that enables us to experience a greater clarity or sense of comprehension. This is accomplished in each case by means of a system of symbols that people have created. In general, the symbol systems differ from the raw experience on which they are superimposed in having an internal order that is inherently simpler than the raw experience. By virtue of this simplicity, the symbol system can provide an order that we can more readily grasp. Lacking this, the symbol system does not meet our needs and it will not survive. The various disciplines vary a bit, of course, in the nature of the symbols they employ and in the kind of order that they effect. They differ too with respect to the kind and amount of participation demanded of the perceiver. Aesthetic symbol products, for example, demand more active, affective participation on the part of the perceiver than do scientific symbol products. This may be more a difference of degree than of kind, however, for in many respects a scientific theory is really a work of art, and it differs from other aesthetic works chiefly in the fact that it is composed of ideas rather than colors, shapes, tones, etc. Even the criteria by which we judge it are more aesthetic in character than most people realize.

If we want to label this basic urge or tendency that leads us to create symbol systems and to seek to experience the order that they provide, there are many motivational constructs we might invoke. We could call it a need for understanding or a need for cognition. It corresponds to what William James and William McDougall called the instinct of curiosity. At the same time, we might view it as a need to control, since the confusion or puzzlement that we seek to relieve through knowledge or symbolic order is accompanied by concern over an inability to cope satisfactorily with events. Once we have arrived at a known or a recognized order, we have a basis for anticipating, predicting, or adjusting to circumstances. We know how to relate to ordered events. It is no accident that we speak of understanding in terms of "grasping" things or, in more contemporary jargon, "getting a handle" on things. The essential equivalence of the need to understand and the need to control may also be seen in the symbol which serves most often in mythology to represent the distinctive achievement of the human species—the symbol of fire. Fire, of course, is both a means of seeing in darkness and a means of transforming things, and it symbolizes both knowledge and the power to create and control.

It is also possible to label the basic prompting underlying science and other disciplines in terms of its characteristic form of expression and to speak of it as a need to symbolize. In doing this, we stress the distinctly human quality of the need. Perhaps we share a need to understand and to control with other species, but symbol-making is clearly a human form of behavior. The production of symbols is so characteristic of the human species that we may regard this tendency as a fundamental instinct in this one creature, an instinct that has developed relatively late in the course of evolution. Indeed, at the human level one might even argue that it functions as a kind of master, or executive, instinct, insofar as it governs the mode of expression of other inborn tendencies.

Symbolizing is probably an inevitable evolutionary consequence of increasing biological complexity. With the level of complexity seen in the human species, there is an increased capacity for inhibition or delayed response. In a creature with a vast behavioral repertoire, delays are bound to occur because there is always a high probability in any given situation that incompatible responses will be jointly evoked. As a consequence, impulses that are readily triggered into action in other species are frequently suppressed or introverted in humans and either denied overt expression or subjected to scheduling and postponement. Thus, the situation that arouses the impulse is likely to culminate in an internal symbolic process in place of a motor act, and any subsequent overt expression is likely to be symbolic in form. Symbolic expression may well be the best place to look for evidence of more specific instinctual tendencies at the human level. The best evidence would be found in the relatively enduring and universal patterns to be found in mythology.

The need to symbolize, then, is at the root of science, but it is a pervasive feature of human existence. To distinguish science from other symbolic enterprises, we must look for something more specific. It is doubtful whether we can find any single criterion that can sharply distinguish science from nonscience. Marx and Hillix review a number of possible criteria that have been proposed for this purpose and conclude that they may all be used to describe science but that none of them does a very satisfactory job of distinguishing science from nonscience.[3] The defining criteria include the purpose of science, its subject matter, the nature of its conclusions, an interest in prediction and control of events, an emphasis on theory, the use of unique and precise terminology, and exactitude. On the whole, Marx and Hillix feel that science is best distinguished by a feature of its method—the use of controlled observation.

It is somewhat less clear whether there is anything distinctive about the symbolic products in which the application of the scientific method culminates. It is commonly believed, at least by lay people, that science has some special concern with truth and that scientific theories differ from other symbol products with respect to objective, factual content. Yet, contrary to popular impressions, most of the things we call theories in science are not composed of factual statements. They are neither summaries of observed fact nor statements of hypothesized fact, though both of these elements may play some part in them. No single position on the nature of scientific theory, however, is generally accepted. There are a number of views on the nature of theory, and there is some corresponding variation in types of theories. To some extent, a position on the nature of theory tends to take the form of a prescription regarding what a theory should be.

Perhaps we can broadly divide the positions on this issue into two classes. On one side are those positions that stress the factual or descriptive content of theories, and on the other are those that stress the creative or constructive aspect of theories. At one extreme, in the first class we have the view of B. F. Skinner, who sees the proper role of theory as the abstract summary of observations and disparages the formal constructions of theorists such as Clark Hull. There are other views within this class that stress the predictive function of theory and hold that theories do and should contain references to hypothetical entities, processes, or relationships that can ultimately be verified by observation. The clearest examples of theories in psychology that fit this formula would be those that contain physiological hypotheses, as in the work of Donald Hebb.

In general, the views in the first class are realistic in the sense that they construe the basic function of a theory as some sort of reproduction of an experienced or experienceable actuality. From the standpoint of those whose views lie in the second class, a theory is more a creative product, a product of invention rather than discovery. It is composed of constructs, or what I have called fictional concepts, that are not assumed to correspond directly to fact.[4] From this standpoint, a theory may be judged in terms of its ability to "explain" a certain range of events in a reasonably simple way and in terms of its potential for stimulating thought and research. It cannot be judged in terms of its descriptive accuracy, but it may be judged in terms of its power to generate predictions. It is my impression that this general position has superseded the realistic one in physics and that it has become increasingly accepted by psychologists during the last few decades.

On the whole, theorists of realistic persuasion probably tend to see a greater difference between scientific theories and other symbol products than do theorists who stress construction, and they tend to prescribe an ideal that will make the difference yet sharper. I believe that the constructive position is more consistent with the actual nature and function of scientific theories, and I do not see this actuality as a condition that either can be or should be remedied. In every effort we make to understand a piece of reality and capture it in symbolic form there are unavoidable elements of simplification, transformation, and construction. Every scientific theory is made by human hands and bears the impress of its creator.

Of all contemporary philosophers, perhaps the one who has best elaborated such a position is Ernst Cassirer.[5] Cassirer might be characterized as a neo-Kantian idealist who is interested in the evolution of the human mind and who treats culture as an expression of that evolution. He holds that all our knowledge of the world and of ourselves rests on an order that the human mind has created in the course of its development. The created order becomes more elaborate as we create new symbols to interpret our experience. This principle applies equally to scientific knowledge, to mythology, and to religion, but between these enterprises there may be differences in awareness regarding the nature and function of symbols. In religion and in the arts, we have long recognized a distinction between the literal and the figurative, and we do not identify symbols with things. In the realm of scientific knowledge we have been slower to recognize the creative nature of our symbolic formulations, but Cassirer apparently sees this recognition as a natural consequence of our continuing mental evolution.

In stressing the constructive nature of our symbolic formulations, we must recognize that the order that we create is not totally arbitrary. We cannot just impose any sort of order on our experience,

and in the realm of scientific statements and theories we expect a
certain kind of fit between the symbol product and the experience to
which it relates. Perhaps there are many possible orders that we can
create that will serve the purpose, but there are infinitely more that
simply will not do. We cannot provide an acceptable theoretical explanation of the outcome of a chemical experiment by reciting "Mary
Had a Little Lamb." In our efforts to symbolize in science, we seem
always to strike a kind of balance between impulses that lead us in
two opposite directions. On the one hand, our symbolizing entails an
effort to discern the nature of a confronted reality and to represent it
faithfully in a scheme that will enable us to cope fully with it.
Perhaps we could describe this as an effort to produce a symbol product that reflects the totality of our experience. On the other hand,
in symbolizing we always make use of symbols and arrangements of
symbols that we already possess, and no matter how novel and complex the given experience or confronted reality, there is usually apparent in our symbolizing an effort to reduce it experientially to
something familiar and simple.

These two facets of symbol-production correspond to the processes that Piaget calls accommodation and assimilation.[6] Piaget regards those two processes as ever-present complementary features of
human perception and thought. Accommodation is a process whereby
we adapt to the requirements or demands that objects, by their nature, impose as we experience them. Assimilation, on the other
hand, is a process whereby we incorporate experiences into intellectual structures that we already possess. Thus accommodation
leads our perception and thought in the direction of the full complexity of the confronted reality, whereas assimilation tends toward reduction to the simple and familiar. The two processes always act
jointly, but at any given time either may carry more weight than
the other.

Piaget first utilized these concepts in his theoretical treatment
of the cognitive and perceptual development of the child. In more
recent work, he applies his developmental concepts to the history of
science. He regards accommodation and assimilation as universal,
inborn processes that operate at all ages. They are as characteristic
of scientific speculation in the adult as they are of the mental processes of the two-year-old. Of course, some structural features of our
cognitive processes undergo developmental change. Piaget describes
several stages in child development. They may be roughly described
on the whole as involving a movement away from a subjective,
egocentric view to one less bound by the child's uniquely individual
experiences and perspective and a movement from an emphasis on

the concrete and immediate to ideas that are more formal, more
abstract, and less tied to immediate situations. Piaget finds essentially the same kinds of trends running through the history of scientific thought. In early stages, thought tends to be characterized by
egocentrism and phenomenism, and these give way to increased construction and reflection. As a result, at a mature stage in scientific
thought, there is less emphasis on the most immediate and obvious
features of experience and a greater awareness of the extent to
which the scientist's own perspective affects his observations. Both
ontogenetically and historically, thought becomes progressively more
complex, because although assimilation continues to operate to the
same extent, the structures to which we assimilate our experience
undergo progressive refinement and elaboration.

However we conceptualize the two opposing trends, it is clear
that they both color our thinking constantly, but not necessarily to
the same degree. As we consider the shifting balance between the
two processes, it seems evident that they serve somewhat different
needs. By reducing an experience to the simple and familiar, we
achieve an immediate reduction in the discomfort occasioned by our
confrontation with something as yet unknown. We can readily assure ourselves that the novel, the complex, the strange set of events
"makes sense" to us. Having successfully grasped it in terms of an
image, a concept, or a pattern that is comfortable and well known,
we can relax. To construct a conceptual scheme that does better justice to the full-blown complexity of the experienced events requires
more effort, but it provides a sounder basis for further interaction. It
places us in a better position to achieve effective control in new
situations that involve similar events, and it may therefore provide
a foundation for greater comfort in the long run.

The importance of a proper balance between the two trends has
been given formal recognition in the criteria employed for the
evaluation of theories. While there is no universally accepted set of
criteria, in the innumerable proposals for evaluative standards that
have been advanced we recurrently find two contrasting themes. On
the one hand, there is a theme expressed in terms of economy,
simplicity, or parsimony. On the other hand, there is a theme that
stresses the adequacy of conceptual elaboration, goodness of fit, or
precision, either with respect to events that have been observed or
events that can be predicted. While most theorists would agree that
both kinds of standards are needed, there is little agreement on the
respective weights that should be attached to them. As I have previously suggested, in the case of factor theories of mental ability, we
can find an array of balances, in theories that vary from over-
simplicity to cumbersome complexity.[7]

Maslow speaks of essentially the same polarity in terms of a need for safety and a need for understanding.[8] He sees both needs as instinctoid in nature, but he regards the need for safety as prepotent. If it has not been adequately met, it prevents the expression of the need for understanding. He describes a number of "cognitive pathologies" that involve an overemphasis on the need for safety. He does not believe that this need should be eliminated, however, for he feels we should avoid both the extremes of overcaution and overimpulsiveness in the formulation of theories. Maslow, too, recognizes the importance of a certain balance. Perhaps we should note that such needs affect much more than the simplicity or complexity of our theories and our tendency to stick to old concepts or devise new ones. They affect the domain of inquiry—our willingness to explore new territories or to deal with broad domains rather than narrow ones. Perhaps the most common expression of an intense need for safety or security in a scholar is a tendency to confine attention to a highly confined and specialized area in which one's authority cannot be questioned.

SPECIFIC PATTERNS OF INQUIRY AND SYMBOLIZATION

A need for safety or security may temper all our efforts, but I have argued that there is one underlying need—to understand, to order, to symbolize—that actually prompts the development of science and all the other major symbolic enterprises of mankind. It is possible, however, to distinguish a number of component tendencies or specific subforms of this general disposition. There are two main ways in which we might proceed to make distinctions. One is in terms of the life situations that provoke symbol-production. The other is in terms of the basic types of symbol products, or patterns of symbolization, that emerge. With respect to either of these modes, innumerable specific systems of classification of components appear to be possible.

If we think of provoking life contexts in which symbol systems arise, it is evident that we can recognize a number of major sources of puzzlement that have haunted humanity in all parts of the world throughout the ages. Perhaps the most fundamental source of puzzlement is simply experienced existence itself. If we were to express this in the form of a question, it would be something on the order of: What and why is everything? If we add to this the question *how*, we have covered the basic traditional ground of philosophy. Our most basic experiences of puzzlement can be expressed most directly as questions that are metaphysical in content—or perhaps we could say more broadly that they are the questions that lie at the root of ontology and of such related realms as epistemology, cosmology, and causality. Although the precise way in which we state, separate, or combine these questions is somewhat arbitrary, the questions themselves are truly recurrent and universal ones, and we must assume that there is something in the nature of people or the human situation in general that leads us to ask them.

Among the questions of particular relevance to psychology are those having to do with the nature of self. Each of us tends at some time to wonder who or what he is and how he happens to experience himself as himself, this particular person in this body. We wonder how we came into being and whether in any sense our being preceded our existence as self-aware creatures. These questions are linked, of course, to more general ontological issues—the nature of being per se, the ultimate nature of the world as a whole, and the nature of space, time, and matter.

The distinction between a self or locus of awareness and that which is not part of the self is accompanied by other related distinctions—in particular, that between mind and matter and that between mind and body. We wonder about the relationships between the components of these polarities. We wonder also about the determination of events, especially those in which we participate or which affect us directly, and we raise questions about causality, will, freedom, and purpose. Equally fundamental are the basic issues of epistemology—what we truly know and how we know—and related issues of meaning and truth.

It is customary to regard such questions as the special domain of philosophers and theologians and outside the concern of people in other fields. It is also fashionable in many circles to regard such questions as unimportant, outmoded, or even meaningless. Many scientists pretend to ignore metaphysical issues, and yet there is really nothing one can do in science without making at least implicit assumptions about some of them. Indeed, it can be argued that all intellectual disciplines exist because they constitute ways of dealing with metaphysical questions. "Dealing with" metaphysical questions, of course, does not necessarily mean attempting directly to answer these questions. The questions are of very profound importance because they express a mystery, a bewilderment, a groping for light that we all experience as human beings, and yet these questions, as questions, tend to be unanswerable. To be sure, people have formulated many answers to them, sometimes as articles of dogma, sometimes as working assumptions adopted for convenience. The questions are not of a kind that permits the discovery of ultimate answers, however, and they always return to haunt us again. For this reason, there are relatively few people who find it rewarding to devote their lives to an attempt to provide direct answers.

Many philosophers devote their careers to working directly with the questions without pretending to offer ultimate answers to them. They are content to submit the questions to analysis and to analyze logically the range of possible answers. The work of the scientist, on the other hand, can be seen generally as an attempt to answer a derivative of a metaphysical question. In the scientist, the initial wonderment tends to be displaced from the metaphysical issue to a scientific problem that lends itself to the achievement of a greater sense of certainty. Thus, the physical scientist turns from the issue of the ultimate nature of being, matter, time, and causality to an investigation of the different forms of matter, to a search for elementary particles, and to an effort to find systematic relationships that can be expressed in equations.

The work of psychologists can be seen as an attempt to deal with derivatives of a number of metaphysical questions. Psychologists in the personality area deal essentially with the puzzle of the self. They may sidestep questions concerning its ultimate nature, its purpose, and the why of our experience of it, but they may attempt to clarify the content of our experience of it and relate this content developmentally to other structures and processes. The issues of cause, will, and purpose are replaced to a great extent with issues in learning and motivation theory that submit to systematic investigation. Issues in the realm of perceptual theory serve a similar role as substitutes for questions about the nature of knowledge, truth, mind, and the relationship between mind and matter. In the field of physiological psychology, we turn from a consideration of the ultimate nature of the relationship between mind and body to an empirical investigation of demonstrable correspondences between mental and physiological events.

Thus, psychologists end up pursuing a great variety of research issues, but surely the very raison d'être for the field of psychology is the great puzzle of human consciousness itself. The broad metaphysical questions we raise regarding this are replaced by broad questions of scientific theory, and these lead in turn to more concrete issues for which relevant research data can be obtained. Presumably the substitutions are prompted by a need for certainty. For the scientist at least, the order disclosed by empirical research satisfies this need better than any answer that might be offered to the prior metaphysical question. In some psychologists, the need for certainty leads to a denial of the very subject matter—conscious human experience—for which the field of psychology was created.

In the view of the writer, then, the many intellectual disciplines have their roots in a limited number of fundamental metaphysical questions that people have raised regarding the world and their place in it. These questions have apparently led to a myriad of symbolic products designed to provide either direct answers to these questions or answers to a host of derivative questions. It is possible, however, that even on the side of symbolic expression, we can find a relatively limited number of patterns underlying the major edifices of human intellectual activity. As we have noted, we tend in symbolizing to try to reduce the complex and the unfamiliar to the simple and familiar, and it is doubtful, despite all our efforts to transform the very questions with which we launch intellectual inquiries, that we ever come up with utterly novel answers. Jung has suggested that "there is not a single important idea or view that does not possess historical antecedents."[9]

It is not too difficult to find recurring themes in human thought. There seem, in fact, to be certain modes of symbolizing that recur in particular existential contexts more or less independently of the given cultural setting. The more fundamental the issue of human experience we are concerned with, the more likely is the answer to assume a form that is universal in character. In the world there are many mythologies, but many of the same symbols and themes reappear without respect for cultural boundary lines. Thus, in all cultures we find creation myths, but recurringly the origin of human beings and their world is accounted for in terms of emergence from darkness or in terms of the union and subsequent separation of world parents. Over and over again in myths, light appears as a symbol of emerging human consciousness, and a major event in the creation myth is the creation of light or an emergence into light. Repeatedly, a preexisting state of undifferentiated awareness is represented by the "round"—in artistic representation, a circle or sphere, and often throughout the world, the symbol of the *uroboros,* the serpent that forms a circle by biting its own tail. The same symbol may serve also to represent an ultimate or future state of integration.

Throughout the world we also find great hero myths, with a surprising number of ingredients that tend to recur. As a precondition for greatness, the hero tends to be depicted as having divine origins. Thus he is typically born of a virgin, having been sired by a divine father. Throughout the world he conquers creatures that may be construed as embodiments of elements in his own makeup, as

forces of nature, and as the weight of parental and societal authority. In slaying a dragon, he establishes his power to control consciously his own destiny. In slaying a mighty father figure, he as-
serts his independence from a traditional order.

It would be a mistake to assume that such recurrences are confined to the realm of mythology, though mythology may provide the
best evidence of the independent appearance of universal thought
forms. It is certainly possible in scientific thought, too, to find evidence of recurring modes of symbolization and evidence of definite
constraints on possible modes of symbolization. Thus, the human
knower appears capable of conceptualizing the material universe as
a continuum or as an otherwise empty space containing discrete particles. Correspondingly, he may view the passage of light as a wave
motion in the continuum or as a stream of particles. Faced with the
inadequacies of each viewpoint, the modern theorist resorts to a
combination of the two basic ideas. It is difficult to say whether we
are confronted here with an inherent limit to the number of possible
ways of conceptualizing such a phenomenon as light or simply a
limitation built into the human symbolizer. Perhaps the question
could best be answered by an intelligent being who was not a
member of this species. There is no doubt, however, that we are
dealing here with recurrent human thought forms.

The two basic physical world views have their counterparts in
the psychological realm. Eastern traditions emphasize universal
mind and tend to view the individual mind as an illusion. Western
traditions more often attribute reality to the discrete individual
mind. The individual mind itself has been regarded alternately as
an inseparable whole and as a composite of numerous discrete bits.
Each of these positions has appeared in many guises throughout the
history of psychology. A similar course may be seen in the perennial
recurrence of mechanical and personal models in the explanation of
certain processes and interactions. In the one case, the mind is viewed as analogous to a physical system, sometimes with properties
that are specifically hydraulic or electronic in nature, sometimes in
the more abstract sense of being characterized by forces and ener-
gies. In the other case, the components of the psyche are viewed as
operating like independent personalities. Either view may last but a
short time in a specific theoretical form, but the underlying models
persist and reappear.

There are still more subtle conceptual tendencies that pervade
psychological theory. Here, as in many other forms of human
thought, we find a tendency to treat nonspatial relations in terms of
spatial metaphors. According to Whorf, this tendency is governed

more by the structure of Indo-European languages than by anything in the way of universal human dispositions.[10] Nevertheless, it pervades psychological theory as we know it, expressed in a relatively small number of basic models. The dimensional and topological models were subjected to elaborate formal treatment in the work of Thurstone and Lewin respectively, but both of these had been employed long before in a less explicit way. They will continue to be employed through the foreseeable future to deal with various quantitative and nonquantitative relationships. A connectional, or conjunctional, model could be said to underlie all forms of learning theory and various other realms of theory as well. The notion of layers or levels is evident in much of our treatment of sequences and serial relationships. Still other spatial models tend to recur in developmental theory. The outer trappings of psychological theory keep changing, but we persist in reemploying a relatively small number of underlying ideas.

If our concern here is with major components or subforms of the human need to symbolize, it should be noted that one additional mode of classifying is in terms of recognized distinctions among disciplines. The traditional classes, such as science, art, religion, and philosophy, and the divisions into recognized fields within these classes provide the basis for a system of classification that embodies simultaneously distinctions with respect to questions pursued and distinctions with respect to modes of symbolization. The boundaries with which we are familiar, however, are largely a matter of Western conventions, and it is likely to prove more valuable in the long run to look for components that have a better claim to universal and, in some sense, "natural" status as component tendencies.

THE SOURCES OF UNIVERSAL PATTERNS
IN HUMAN SYMBOL-PRODUCTION

Universally recurring patterns of symbolism constitute the essential empirical basis for Jung's concept of the archetype. From a Jungian standpoint, the recurrence is dependent on a biologically based tendency common to the species or to a large segment of the species. Critics of the archetype concept have sometimes accused Jung of having a very low threshold for perceiving similarity, but no one can fail to be impressed by the scope of his examination of human symbolism. Whatever flaws may be revealed in Jung's doctrine of the archetypes and the collective unconscious, it is likely to stand as one of the major intellectual achievements by an individual in this century.

In defense of the Jungian position, we may note that Jung's theory does not make naive assumptions about universal symbolism. It does not require precise symbol identities, since it is the underlying archetype that is alleged to be universal. The symbol as an expression of the archetype is subject to fluctuation. For another thing, Jungian theory assumes that what is differentiated as a distinguishable archetype in the collective unconscious depends on developments that occur in the conscious mind. Hence, the expression of archetypes is subject to some cultural variation and to progression over time within a given cultural setting.

To the extent that we do find good evidence of universal patterns in symbolization, there are basically two lines of explanation we might pursue to account for them—a common biological basis and a common basis in inevitable human experience. Some sort of biological basis seems most probable for those tendencies in human thought that are most truly universal. Such tendencies are likely at the same time to be among the most difficult to recognize because we take them for granted. They provide such a persistent ground for our thoughts that we have nothing with which to contrast them, and we fail to recognize that thought might occur without them. Examples might be our very tendency to impose order of some kind on our experience, to make distinctions or formulate dichotomies, and to experience the world as made up of discrete things.

Our quest for order achieves its most direct expression when we are able to experience certain fairly simple forms that we regard as ideal or perfect without having to bend or mutilate them through a process of accommodation. Under appropriate conditions, the uncontaminated form may be a source of profound aesthetic or spiritual experience. We often think of the search for ideal forms as an aim of the arts, but there is much evidence that philosophers, mathematicians, and scientists have engaged in a similar quest, and Edna St. Vincent Millay tells us that "Euclid alone has looked on Beauty bare." An effort to find ideal intellectual forms that transcend particular domains is prominent among the thinkers in an idealistic tradition that includes such men as Pythagoras, Plato, Copernicus, and Kepler. To some extent, the experience sought over centuries by alchemists and symbolized to a degree by gold represents a parallel endeavor.

The search for transcendent intellectual forms even provides the theme for a major novel of our time—Hermann Hesse's *Glasperlenspiel*. It would obviously be a mistake to assume that this search is merely an outmoded game of past centuries in science, since every theorist appears to be motivated by the hope that he will find a relatively simple form that will provide the key to understanding a realm that appears initially to be very complex and disorderly. If possible, too, we prefer theories of broad scope—theories that embody transcendent form to the extent that they are not confined in application to a very limited set of phenomena. Thus, the construction of a unified general field theory has been a major goal for many contemporary physicists. A similar motive surely underlies the efforts of numerous scientists and philosophers to extract or devise a set of basic principles common to diverse scientific domains—as seen in such noteworthy examples as cybernetics,[11] general system theory,[12] and information theory.[13]

The insistent way in which human beings have engaged in this kind of search over the ages strongly suggests that they have an inborn bent to achieve the kind of experience that is provided by simple symbolic forms. Jung would have us believe that some of these symbolic forms—such as the quanternity, the trinity, and the circle or mandala—may individually have special archetypal foundations and that they are recurrently employed for this reason. This is more difficult to judge, since their elementary character itself would tend to favor their frequent occurrence in symbolic productions. To expose yet one more facet of this issue, we should probably note that the Jungian doctrine of the archetypes is itself an expression of an idealistic quest for transcendent form in symbol systems.

The notion of inevitable human experience seems a little more tenable than the idea of strict biological determination as an explanation for many specific instances of universal symbolism. Thus, the fact that fire functions throughout the world as a symbol of emotion and as a symbol of knowledge and creative power can easily be related to our common experience with fire. Wherever people deal with fire, they discover that contact with it is very exciting, that it provides light, and that it transforms things. The use of water as a symbol of the unknown or unconscious realm, sometimes the realm to which we go at death, is also consistent with our common experience. Water is semitransparent, and in large bodies it conceals things that may nonetheless move around within its depths. Unlike the solid ground, it may be easily penetrated—one may move readily into a region out of sight, and one may die in the process.

The creation myth makes use of common observations regarding the origin of individuals. Thus, the creation of humanity and the advent of human consciousness are ascribed to a process like that of the newborn that emerges from the womb. To the extent that people in a given society recognize a causal relationship between the sex act and reproduction, the myth may make use of two parent figures, usually heaven and earth as father and mother respectively.

The tendency to explain the mysteries of the world by analogy to the most familiar experiences that seem formally comparable is certainly not confined to the realm of mythology. According to the root-metaphor theory of Pepper, every basic metaphysical position—or world hypothesis—rests on an analogy to some area of common-sense fact.[14] This view seems to apply equally well to the most fundamental ideas or models on which scientific theories are erected. Thus, our two basic ways of interpreting light correspond to the two basic ways in which we directly observe the transmission of effects across distances—the movement of bodies from one place to another and the displacement of intervening media. It is likely that in the most abstract forms of psychological theory we can never completely avoid at least implicit metaphorical reference to familiar physical events and physical spaces. The very structure of our language is sufficient to guarantee such references as an unavoidable connotative overtone to theoretical formulations.

The main point of the present discussion, in any case, is that certain common human tendencies, including some features of the symbolization process per se as well as many specific forms of symbolism, enter into all intellectual disciplines from the most ancient to the most modern. To an extent, we may attribute these to biologically determined predispositions. To an extent, we may attribute them to experiences that inevitably occur in all parts of the world. These two explanations, of course, are not mutually exclusive. The latter necessarily presupposes some common species properties that make universal experience and expression possible. So far as we know, fire and water do not have quite the same symbolic properties for any other species.

Various interactions between the two presumed sources of universal effects are possible. Given a biological determinant, some sort of imprinting may be required for its development. Furthermore, forces within a given culture may either capitalize on the biological determinant or operate in such a way as to suppress its expression. For that matter, the actual use and form of any symbol are necessarily always affected by diverse factors within the culture in which it appears. It is for this reason that evidence for archetypes must be sought in cross-cultural symbolic congruences rather than in symbolic identities.

Since specific forms of symbolic expression are subject to cross-cultural variation and to evolution within a given culture, we might ask whether it is not possible to arrive at symbol systems that transcend the modes of experiencing, thinking, and organizing peculiar to Homo sapiens the symbol-maker, systems that do not bear the stamp of a particular species. Bertalanffy sees the possibility of a "progressive deanthropomorphization" of scientific concepts and a gradual emergence of scientific theory that would transcend the psychophysical constitution of its creators and be more "universally committal."[15] Perhaps the theory of relativity and quantum theory are major steps in such a direction. Of course, the very fact that scientific theory tends to evolve in such a direction is itself an expression of an impulse peculiar to our species, for it is but one instance of a pervasive tendency of human beings to try to surmount their biological limitations.

THE PROSPECTS FOR RESEARCH ON THE PSYCHOLOGICAL FOUNDATIONS OF SCIENCE

The achievement of a better understanding of the psychological roots of science and of that distinctive part of science known as psychology requires more thorough analysis, both logical and empirical, of the subject matter we have been discussing than anyone has yet attempted. We appear to be confronted with a multivariate problem that lends itself to conceptualization in terms of a hierarchical model. It is meaningful to think of the roots of science in terms of one basic human tendency, which we have characterized in terms of a need to understand, to control, or to symbolize. This tendency seems to underlie not only science but art, philosophy, religion, and mythology as well.

This unitary view of human symbolic systems represents a high degree of abstraction from observed symbolic activities. It corresponds to the most general level, i.e., the highest level or peak, of a hierarchy of description and interpretation. It is equally possible to think of this tendency in terms of a number of distinguishable subforms. We may separate these in terms of the different phases of human experience that provoke symbol production, in terms of different modes of symbolization, or in terms of some combination of these two things. It is possible in turn to analyze the subforms into still finer subdivisions. We have already suggested that with respect to provoking experiences, broad metaphysical questions might be considered subforms of the basic general need. The basic questions of science may be regarded as corresponding to a third level of the hierarchy in the sense that they may be viewed as derivatives of the metaphysical questions and are more numerous and specific in character. Among the scientific questions themselves, we may obviously distinguish many degrees of generality and specificity.

The highest level of the hierarchy is necessarily the most universal, for here we are concerned with a human tendency that is obviously common to people of all cultures. It is possible that no matter how we proceed to determine the ingredients of different levels of the hierarchy we will be dealing with progressively less universal tendencies as we move toward greater specificity. At the base of the hierarchy, we would find specific questions raised by few people and specific features of symbol products that would not occur widely.

One basic way of illuminating further the psychological roots of science would be to ascertain in a more definitive way the components of the hierarchy. To define these components on various levels in terms of the experiential contexts that lead to symbolization would seem to call primarily for logical analysis of the questions people ask and of their interrelationships. The symbol products of mankind may also be subjected to logical analysis and classification.

There are certain features of human symbol production, however, that seem to call for a more empirical type of analysis. This seems particularly necessary for those features of symbolization that have been alleged to rest on a collective or archetypal basis. For these, the crucial evidence would seem to consist of recurring concordances of symbol and context—repeated instances in which a given symbol or set of symbols is invoked as a way of dealing with a particular aspect of human experience. The Jungian doctrine of archetypes rests largely on such observed recurrences in folklore, occult systems of thought, and dreams. It remains to be seen to what extent such recurrences can be found in systems of a more scientific character.

There is an evident need for a more systematic procedure for identifying recurrent patterns of symbolization. Even if we could afford to wait for occasional geniuses of Jungian caliber to come along and scan the whole realm of human thought for us, we are not likely to agree readily on their judgments regarding the recurrent patterns. Perhaps someone will ultimately devise a satisfactory procedure for assessing systematically the similarity of symbol products. Such a procedure, however, is not likely to provide a basis for making simple categorical judgments about whether a set of products either does or does not point to a common underlying archetype. More likely, we must be prepared to think of any given class of symbol products in terms of a similarity hierarchy. Thus, in certain ways all creation myths are alike, but we might also regard them as falling into, say, four main classes as we attend to certain distinguishing features. As we attend to more details, these classes can be further subdivided. A systematic method for assessing symbol concomitances might provide a basis for stating more precisely the degree of universality of various features of symbol products.

Once we have obtained a more definitive picture of the basic and recurring pattern of symbolization in science, of course, it is easier to deal with various questions concerning the determinants of these patterns. The matter of species-specific biological roots is only one such question. It would also be important to relate symbolic patterns to cognitive and perceptual processes, to the structure of the languages employed by theorists, and to patterns of social influence.

2. Diverging Pathways in Psychology

THE CHOICE OF A DISCIPLINE

In the first chapter I was mainly concerned with the ground common to all sciences, or to humanity's symbolic enterprises in general. While these all have certain common psychological roots, there are obviously factors that make for divergences in focus and orientation. There are some divergences that follow national or cultural lines, but there are also diverging patterns that cross-cut cultural boundaries, and there are diverging paths that form within specific groups and specific disciplines. These are all of potential interest to a psychology of science.

The factors that determine the choice of a particular discipline have long been of widespread interest because anyone who is confronted with the choice of a professional career must wrestle with these factors within himself. Intellectual disciplines vary with respect to the basic metaphysical puzzles that underlie them, with respect to the transformations applied to these underlying issues (transformations that determine the issues to which the discipline is explicitly addressed), and with respect to the modes of symbolic production and manipulation employed. Because of these variations, different disciplines impose somewhat different requirements with respect to the talents, interests, and temperaments of those who would seek admission to them.

The Western world has long recognized a fundamental distinction between the natural sciences (and related technical professions) on the one hand and the arts or humanities on the other. Popular speculation regarding the temperament of the artist and the poet and the mentality of the physical scientist and the engineer has long been commonplace, but solid research on the psychological characteristics of people in different disciplines remains at a rather primitive level. Perhaps the best demonstrated findings are those pertaining to ability patterns, but even here the evidence is largely of a practical kind. It provides a better basis for vocational guidance and occupational selection than for an understanding of cognitive-process patterns. Nevertheless, the available evidence offers a broad basis for predicting differences that have not yet been examined directly, and there are promising beginnings, such as the research of Hudson, who has found that students in the sciences tend to emphasize convergent thinking while those in the arts tend to emphasize divergent thinking.[1]

Probably no contemporary statement of differences between people in the sciences and people in the humanities has aroused more comment and controversy than C. P. Snow's little book on the "two cultures."[2] Snow actually focuses rather narrowly on people in the physical sciences and engineering in the one case and "literary intellectuals" in the other case, and his observations are based on what he sees in English society and have little, if any, applicability to other countries. He sees a regrettable lack of communication, even hostility, between the two groups. Each group has a stereotyped view of the other. The literary intellectuals see scientists as brash, boastful, shallowly optimistic, and unaware of the general condition of humanity, while the scientists see the literary intellectuals as lacking in foresight, unconcerned with their fellow humans, anti-intellectual in a deep sense, and anxious to restrict both art and thought to the existential moment. The sort of gulf that Snow describes seems to be tied to features peculiar to British society, particularly a high degree of specialization in higher education, and some critics feel that even with respect to England, Snow has exaggerated the split. In any case, Snow suggests that the intellectual world is divided into two mutually isolated groups of people, and in elaborating on this thesis he indeed focuses on two groups rather widely separated in their interests, but he pays scant attention to the many groups, particularly the social scientists, whose interests in many respects lie in between.

Snow does not attempt to give us a very clear picture of the actual psychological differences between the two groups. There are others who have offered more ideas on fundamental differences between major disciplines. Royce, for example, has suggested differences in the use of four fundamental epistemologies, or ways of knowing.[3] The four epistemologies that he distinguishes are rationalism, intuitionism, empiricism, and authoritarianism. He believes that mathematics and philosophy stress rationalism, while art stresses intuitionism, and science stresses a combination of rationalism and empiricism. These alignments rest on rather obvious demands imposed by these disciplines on those who pursue them, but even apart from their work, the people who enter these various disciplines may differ basically in their approaches to reality. Common sense suggests this, and some of Royce's research supports the idea.

To a psychology of psychology, of course, it is of particular interest to know why people choose careers in psychology. There is a popular notion, often expressed with a light touch of derision, that the people who choose psychology for a career do so because they have emotional problems and hope that in this field they may find a way to solve them. I once heard Edward Tolman comment on this point. He said that, of course, the popular view was correct, for it is the individual who experiences emotional disturbance and who is thereby motivated to look inside and try to figure out what makes things tick who becomes a psychologist. But then, Tolman pointed out, there are other people who are also emotionally disturbed but who tend to project the disturbance out onto society, and such folk enter the various other social sciences. And then there are still others who cannot bear to face the disturbance in any form, either within or projected without, and these are the people who enter the physical sciences. This particular analysis actually originated as a family joke—in fact in a conversation with his admired older brother, an eminent atomic physicist. While Tolman obviously offered this formulation in jest, I do not know whether he considered it complete nonsense. There is undoubtedly a kernel of truth to it, for we are all subject to emotional problems of one kind or another, and we cultivate individual modes of dealing with them. Our vocational choices are bound to reflect these modes to some degree. I think that when psychologists are faced with personal problems, they are more inclined than most people to deal with them with a sort of obsessive introspection combined with intellectualization. Their training tends to encourage this, and the field probably draws people who are already inclined to function in this way. Like just about any style of adjustment, this one has both merits and drawbacks.

Psychology by its nature is the domain of the introspective individual. Traditionally it is the science of the mind. Every discipline seeks to make sense of the contents of human experience, but psychology is the discipline that exists in order to make sense of the fact of experience itself. Psychology comes into being when, puzzled by our experience, we proceed to raise questions about the experiencer and about the process of experiencing.

At the heart of psychology are such issues as the nature of mind, the relation of mind to body and to matter in general, and the

nature and origin of the self as an individual experiencing being. To
be sure, many psychologists deny any concern with such issues, and
some would contend that these issues are meaningless. At least in
an historical sense, psychology is undeniably the supremely introverted science, the science directly concerned with the subjective
realm. Yet it is in the discipline now known as psychology that we
find the greatest number of vocal antisubjectivists (along with a sizable number who represent the traditional emphasis).

The presence of the antisubjectivist in psychology poses interesting questions for which clear answers do not yet exist. We could
argue that psychology today encompasses much more than its traditional concerns. Thus, its various areas simply draw many individuals who at an earlier time would have gone into other fields. It is
also conceivable, however, that almost everyone who becomes a
psychologist starts with a concern over the great puzzle of human
consciousness but ultimately copes with the concern in a way
governed by his own temperament. Thus, the antisubjectivist denies
his original concern because a continuing preoccupation with it does
not suit his essentially extraverted bent or because he has a strong
need for certainty.

Obviously an examination of the discipline itself tells us something about the people who become psychologists, but it leaves some
questions unanswered. We have a certain amount of empirical information about the characteristics of psychologists. Perhaps the
best known research is that of Roe, who studied eminent men in
several different branches of science—physics, biology, anthropology,
and psychology.[4] She analyzed demographic, biographical, and
psychometric data. On the whole, her data tell us more about the
characteristics of eminent men than about the distinctive characteristics of psychologists, but she did find some differences between
sciences. The social scientists (psychologists and anthropologists)
proved to be more verbally productive than the biologists and physicists on such tests as the TAT and Rorschach, and they showed more
evidence of a concern with social relationships. Among the physicists
and biologists, there was greater evidence of shyness and social isolation in the childhood years. On the other hand, some of Roe's data
(such as her findings for Rorschach movement responses) are consistent with the idea that the social scientists tended as a group to be
more introverted in the Jungian sense than the physicists and
biologists. That is, they were more introverted in the sense of being
more concerned with the subjective realm, though more extraverted
in the sense that they were more involved with other people.

In a study comparing 20 graduate students in clinical psychology with 20 graduate students in physics, Galinsky obtained biog-

raphical data that bear a clear parallel to those of Roe.[5] In several respects, the physics students were found to be more socially isolated as children. As children, psychology students had warmer and closer relationships with their mothers, they had more opportunity to be curious about interpersonal matters, they had more peer relationships, and they more often had strong but conflictful attachments to their families. There were also differences in the discipline received in childhood. For the physics students, it tended to be rigid, to stress obedience, and to be meted out by fathers. For the psychology students, it tended to be more flexible, to stress an appeal to feelings, and to be meted out by mothers.

Cattell and Drevdahl have also reported data that tend to support Roe's findings.[6] They present findings on the Sixteen Personality Factor Questionnaire for a fairly sizable sample of eminent biologists, physicists, and psychologists. The trends for the eminent-scientist group as a whole are a bit more striking than the differences between the fields of science. On the whole, the scientists tended to be relatively stable and free of anxiety. In most but not all respects, they showed a pattern of social introversion. One might briefly characterize the scores in the introversion-extraversion realm by saying that the typical subject in the sample does not fear social interaction and freely engages in it when necessary but that he tends to be rather self-sufficient and has a relatively low need for social contact. Other characteristics common to all three groups of eminent scientists were high intelligence, emotional sensitivity, and a tendency toward radical and unconventional modes of thought.

Since very similar scores were later found in a group of prominent artists and writers,[7] it seems likely that we are seeing here a pattern characteristic of creative people in our society, rather than one confined to scientists. The psychologists, of course, proved to be more similar to the other groups of scientists than they were to the general population. They differed, however, in being somewhat less socially introverted on the average than the physicists and biologists and in being somewhat more radical and unconventional in their thinking. The available information on various kinds of scientists remains very limited in scope. There is a need, in particular, for data on samples that are more broadly representative of the people in such fields as psychology, anthropology, physics, and biology.

PATTERNS OF ORIENTATION IN PSYCHOLOGY

Psychology itself is a highly diversified discipline. There are now a number of distinct specialty areas within psychology, and

their separation has gradually increased in recent years. Most
graduate programs demand some breadth in the training of the student, but it is nonetheless possible to find physiological psychologists
who know practically nothing about social psychology and clinical
psychologists who know practically nothing about animal behavior. I
am more interested, however, in another kind of division that is to
some degree associated with the area division—a division according
to patterns of theoretical orientation or outlook. Here the subcategories are probably less clear than they used to be, because
there was a time when psychologists were more inclined to associate
themselves with well-defined schools of thought. Today the faithful
partisans are outnumbered by theoretical eclectics, but the result is
certainly not a homogeneous climate. There is marked diversity, and
it is difficult to identify and distinguish common patterns of orientation with any clarity. The nature of patterns of orientation has long
been a popular topic of conversation among psychologists, but it is
only in recent years that there has been any effort to subject the
matter to systematic research.

Most often speculative treatments of orientation patterns in
psychology employ a grand dichotomy of some sort. It is usually cast
these days in terms of a division between the behaviorists and the
humanists—or possibly a three-way split if humanistic psychology is
seen as a "third force" in contrast to both behaviorism and
psychoanalysis. Something like the behaviorism-humanism distinction has been proposed in many other guises. In 1961, Rogers spoke of
two basic trends in present-day American psychology.[8] One was an
objective trend characterized by hardheadedness, reductionist theory,
operational definitions, objective methods, and an emphasis on the
concrete and specific. The other was an existential trend, which was
concerned with the experiencing person and with the whole spectrum of human behavior.

Gordon Allport speaks of much the same division in terms of
Lockean and Leibnitzean traditions, thus giving the dichotomy a little more historical footing.[9] He believes it is possible to trace a tradition that has predominated in Anglo-American psychology to John
Locke. Running through this tradition is a stress on the reactive
organism, the idea that the human being is essentially a passive
recipient and reactor to impinging environmental events. Allport
sees environmentalism, behaviorism, S-R psychology, positivism, operationism, elementarism, and the use of mathematical models as
expressions of this tradition. The Leibnitzean tradition, which owes
more to the thinking of Leibnitz and Kant, has predominated in continental European psychology. In this tradition, the organism is

viewed as more active and self-propelled. Gestalt psychology, phenomenology, and various related holistic or molar psychologies are outgrowths of this tradition.

Essentially the same dichotomy appears in many other forms— but with a recognizable reassembling of most of the same ingredients. In a paper on holism, Ansbacher distinguishes two basic viewpoints which he calls the elementaristic and the holistic.[10] The first is said to be generally associated with determinism, mechanism, reductionism, and the espousal of a "spectator" theory of knowledge (an idea close to that of the reactive organism), while the holistic position is said to be accompanied in general by an emphasis on becoming, creativity, growth, and self-actualization and by a conception of the learner as a concerned participant in the learning process. Still earlier, we find a similar distinction made by Murray between peripheralists and centralists in psychology.[11] And though the parallel is not quite as close, it is still unmistakably present in William James' famous distinction between toughminded and tenderminded philosophers.[12]

There is much agreement among these dichotomizing treatments of psychological theory. Yet in the two packages of variables that are alleged to belong to the two basic camps in psychology, we find an assortment of features that do not really go together out of logical necessity. Indeed, while it is easy to think of individual theorists who clearly belong to one or the other of the two camps, it is also easy to think of many others who do not—theorists who combine the features of humanism and behaviorism, or the Lockean and Leibnitzean traditions, in ways that defy the general rule. Thus, there is reason to wonder whether we can satisfactorily describe variations in theoretical orientation in psychology in terms of one grand dimension.

Brunswik, who provides a more sophisticated treatment of the matter than most other writers, insists on a two-dimensional scheme.[13] He distinguishes two basic issues in psychological theory. One is concerned with the rigor of fact finding, inference, and communication, or with what we might call the quest for certainty. According to Brunswik, there are essentially two ways of handling this issue. One solution is subjectivistic, mentalistic, and "introspectionistic," while the other is objectivistic. The other basic issue is the level of complexity of theory. Here the basic choice is between the holistic and the elementaristic, or in the terms used by Brunswik and by Tolman, the molar and the molecular. Thus, Brunswik describes two basic polarities—subjectivism-objectivism and holism-elementarism—which he views as independent on both logical and historical grounds. He apparently sees a clear geographical division only with respect to the first. Thus, objectivism is seen in the empiricism and positivism that have been prevalent in England and the United States, while subjectivism is seen in the raionalism and idealism long prevalent on the European continent. The other writers I have noted tend to collapse the two polarities into one and see a link between objectivism and elementarism and between subjectivism and holism. On purely logical grounds, Brunswik's view seems the more defensible one, for the two polarities do represent issues that are logically separable. On the other hand, we can undoubtedly find a historical basis for arguing that the two polarities have in fact been intertwined. If we are interested in precision of historical description, then the degree of intertwining is an important consideration.

As I suggested in Chapter 1, our desire for conceptual simplicity often works at odds with an effort to achieve precise description. If we want to deal with patterns of theoretical orientation in a more precise way, we will probably need to recognize a greater number of fundamental and independent issues than the two that Brunswik has noted. It is rather easy to identify other issues that are fairly independent of these. Indeed, it takes only a casual glance through an assortment of psychology textbooks to discover a variety of issues that psychologists have considered fundamental. There is the nature-nurture issue. There is the question of free will (vs. a determinism defined in such a way as to exclude it). There is the issue of the moral quality of basic human nature—whether it is assumed to be good, bad, or neutral. There are issues pertaining to the use of various kinds of theoretical models and modes of description. It is easy to list dozens of terms that have been employed to label basic issues in psychological theory.

One of the more comprehensive listings of fundamental issues is presented by Watson, who lists eighteen pairs of contrasting "prescriptions" that have guided theory and research in psychology for extended periods of time.[14] His prescriptions are as follows:

1. Conscious mentalism vs. unconscious mentalism
2. Contentual objectivism vs. contentual subjectivism
3. Determinism vs. indeterminism
4. Empiricism vs. rationalism
5. Functionalism vs. structuralism
6. Inductivism vs. deductivism
7. Mechanism vs. vitalism
8. Methodological objectivism vs. methodological subjectivism

9. Molecularism vs. molarism
10. Monism vs. dualism
11. Naturalism vs. supernaturalism
12. Nomotheticism vs. idiographicism
13. Peripheralism vs. centralism
14. Purism vs. utilitarianism
15. Quantitativism vs. qualitativism
16. Rationalism vs. irrationalism
17. Staticism vs. developmentalism
18. Staticism vs. dynamicism

This is a fairly inclusive list, but it does not exhaust the issues that have been viewed as important and basic. A truly comprehensive list would be lengthy, but it would also be a bit redundant. We cannot carry a list very far before someone is bound to contend that we have introduced too much overlap or that a certain issue is adequately covered by some combination of other issues on the list. There is an obvious value in including a sufficient variety of variables to provide fairly precise description or characterization for any given theorist. Yet there is also a value in reducing the list to a small number of variables which is adequate for the purpose and which contains those variables that we can somehow view as most fundamental.

There are essentially two ways in which we might proceed toward such a goal (an economical list of fundamental issues) once we have assembled a list that seems to cover the total territory. One route is logical analysis and the other is empirical analysis. Logical analysis is a bit hazardous in this case because we are dealing with a large number of rather elastic variables. Even if we can agree on an initial set of carefully defined variables, there is certainly no simple deductive procedure that will yield a universally acceptable result. In a way, the numerous writers who have presented their views on the basic issues in psychology have done their own independent logical analyses and have certainly failed to arrive at a common agreement as to *the* most fundamental issues. The strategy I have employed in my own research depends more heavily on empirical analysis. The basic idea is simply to assess a large number of psychologists with respect to their positions on a large number of issues and then determine which positions go with which. An examination of the correlations among the variables by such procedures as factor analysis leads to the isolation of a relatively small number of dimensions that can be used to describe all the patterns of theoretical orientation that have been observed. This empirical-statistical mode of analysis is not necessarily superior to the sort of

logical analysis employed by, say, Brunswik, and it will not necessarily yield the same kind of result. It is my impression, however,
that it has yielded dimensions that make sense both in terms of historical associations among the variables they embrace and in terms
of "inherent" relationships among those variables. In short, it has
yielded dimensions that should agree with the results of *some* kind
of logical analysis of the domain.

AN ANALYTIC SEARCH FOR BASIC DIMENSIONS OF ORIENTATION

For my own preliminary attempt to isolate basic dimensions of
theoretical orientation, I first tried to assemble a comprehensive list
of variables that might distinguish theorists of differing outlook.[15] I
consulted a great variety of published works in an effort to identify
variables that had been used to distinguish major positions within
psychology as a whole and within major areas of psychology. The
result was a list of several dozen items. I proceeded to prune this
down to a more manageable list—a list that could conveniently be
used to rate a number of major theorists. I eliminated obvious dupli-
cations. My aim at this point was a list that would be reasonably
economical but still comprehensive. It seemed essential to cover
every important variable that could be applied to all psychological
theorists, but to eliminate variables that would be meaningful only
within very limited areas of theory. I tried to avoid words that were
vague or ambiguous or had more than one distinct meaning, such as
empirical or *objective,* while still covering the ground that they represented. I also wanted to formulate the list in such a way that each
item would be fairly clearly ratable and would represent a reasonably distinct variable. I tried to avoid any unnecessary assumptions
about inherent relationships or polarities among variables—e.g., an
assumption that holistic formulations necessarily preclude an elementaristic focus or that a nomothetic emphasis is necessarily opposed to a concern with individuality or individual uniqueness.

It is apparent that the notion of theoretical orientation encompasses many different kinds of variables. It includes philosophical
assumptions and it includes biases that affect the subject matter on
which one focuses attention, the way in which one gathers information, and the manner in which one formulates theory. In the work of
the psychologist, these areas are so closely interwoven that we cannot deal with one without touching on the others. The content on
which one chooses to focus inevitably affects one's choice of research
methods, and it may affect the kind of theory that it is possible to
construct. It is possible, however, to think of the 34 variables that

were ultimately included in my list as falling into four broad categories, depending on whether they are primarily concerned with content emphasis, methodological emphasis, basic assumptions, or mode of conceptualization. The 34 variables are as follows:

CONTENT EMPHASIS

1. Learning
2. Sensation and perception
3. Motivation
4. Conscious processes, conscious experience
5. Observable behavior, action, performance
6. Unconscious processes
7. Emotion
8. Self-concept, self-perception
9. Biological determinants of behavior
10. Social determinants of behavior
11. Heredity, constitution
12. Influence of past experience on behavior
13. Immediate external determinants of behavior
14. Total organization of behavior
15. Uniqueness of individual personality
16. Persisting traits of individuals

METHODOLOGICAL EMPHASIS

17. Introspective reports of experience
18. Rigidly controlled experimentation
19. Statistical analysis
20. "Armchair" speculation
21. Naturalistic observation

BASIC ASSUMPTIONS

22. Voluntarism, viewpoint that volition or will is a central feature in mental processes and constitutes an independent influence on behavior
23. Determinism, viewpoint that behavior is completely explicable in terms of antecedent events
24. Finalism, teleology, viewpoint that ends or purposes have a causal influence on behavior
25. Mechanism, viewpoint that all activities and processes are completely explicable in terms of the laws of physical mechanics

MODE OF CONCEPTUALIZATION

26. Operational definition of concepts
27. Elementarism, atomism, description or analysis of events in terms of relatively small units
28. Holism, totalism, treatment of phenomena in relatively global terms
29. Nomothetic approach, formulation of general principles
30. Normative generalization, statistical generalizations about groups of people
31. Quantitative formulation of principles and relationships
32. Quantitative description of individuals and behavior
33. Conceptualization in terms of hypothetical entities
34. Use of analogies based on physical systems

If major theorists were to be assessed in terms of these variables, it was obviously necessary to decide which theorists to use. Here I relied on data that Salvatore Zagona and I had reported earlier.[16] To identify major theorists, we had asked a large number of judges to rate 142 psychological theorists with respect to the overall importance of their theoretical contributions and with respect to the importance of their contributions during each decade in which they were active from the 1880s to the 1950s. For purposes of the research on theoretical orientation, I looked for those theorists who emerged among the top 50 with respect to mean ratings for overall contributions and those who emerged among the top 10 for each decade. By including every theorist who met either one of these criteria, I arrived at a list of 54 theorists.

Given a list of theorists and a list of variables, the next task was to assess each theorist on each of the variables. The ideal procedure would entail a thorough content analysis of the published works of each theorist, but I resorted again to the easier route of securing ratings from presumed experts. For this purpose, I compiled a list of 232 correspondents. This list was composed of psychologists known either to have taught a course in the history of psychology or to have an interest in history and systems. An initial list derived through reference to college and university catalogs and by reference to entries in the APA Directory was supplemented by names obtained through personal contact or through correspondence with others.

My correspondents were undoubtedly better qualified for this task than a random sample of psychologists would have been, but they were still subject to rating biases. At the least, it would have been desirable to hold these constant across all ratings by asking each judge to provide a complete set of ratings on all theorists. For two obvious reasons, however, this was not practical. For one thing, I sensed that the prospect of supplying 1836 ratings would seem much too formidable to most raters. Furthermore, it is not reasonable to assume that any one rater would have sufficient knowledge of all the theorists to be able to rate them all competently. Therefore, I simplified the rater's task first of all by dividing the list of theorists into three subgroups. Each of my correspondents received a form that contained the names of only 18 theorists. Within that set the rater was permitted to confine ratings to those theorists with whom he or she was most familiar. For these theorists, however, a complete set of ratings was requested. As a consequence, each theorist was assessed by a somewhat different set of raters, and it was possible for a theorist to be assessed by few or many raters. The actual number of complete sets of ratings varied from 6 for Charcot to 38 for Freud (which perhaps indicates how successfully Freud managed to eclipse the idol of his youth). The average number of complete sets was about 20 per theorist.

To arrive at a single score on each variable for each theorist, I took the mean of all available ratings. I thus obtained a 54 × 34 score matrix. From this I derived the intercorrelations among the variables. Centroid extraction applied to the correlation matrix yielded six factors, which I rotated to the best approximation to oblique simple structure. It is possible to express an oblique solution in more than one way. Both the factor structure matrix and the factor pattern matrix are desirable for interpretive purpose, and I derived both of these. The former contains the correlations between the individual variables and the factors, while the latter contains factor loadings. The correlations show to what extent a factor actually shares variance with each variable, but the factor loadings provide a somewhat clearer picture of the set of variables that is best aligned with each factor in factor space.

In the lists presented below, I have indicated after each variable, in parentheses, first its loading for the given factor and then its correlation with the factor. Let me assure the non-factor-analyst reader that these fine points are not terribly essential for a basic grasp of the present findings. We can think of each one of the factors as a kind of ideal variable that represents an important mode of variation in theoretical orientation. There are six of these ideal variables altogether. Each is fairly independent of the others, and together they pretty well capture the information provided by the 34

variables. We can largely predict and account for a theorist's standing on any of the original 34 variables by noting where he stands on
the six ideal variables, or factors.

To understand or interpret any given factor, we need primarily
to note which variables relate to it strongly in a positive way and
which ones relate to it strongly in a negative way. The factor represents essentially whatever is common to these variables (but not
common to the remaining variables). We can think of it as a dimension which at one pole represents what is common to the positively
related variables and which at the other pole represents what is
common to the negatively related variables.

FACTOR 1

Positive variables:
    4. Conscious processes (1.07, .92)
   17. Introspective reports (.96, .96)
   22. Voluntarism (.81, .92)
   24. Finalism (.76, .86)
   20. "Armchair" speculation (.70, .87)
    2. Sensation and perception (.55, .31)
    6. Unconscious processes (.54, .66)
    8. Self-concept (.55, .76)
   33. Hypothetical entities (.54, .26)

Negative variables:
    5. Observable behavior (−.95, −.84)
   23. Determinism (−.60, −.82)
   25. Mechanism (−.57, −87)
   26. Operational definition (−.57, −.85)
    9. Biological determinants (−.43, −.37)
    1. Learning (−.39, −.67)
   13. Immediate external determinants (−.35, −.59)

There is an additional bit of information derivable from the data
that can aid us in interpretation. For each of the 54 theorists I obtained a set of factor scores by use of multiple-regression weights.
The theorists who scored very high on factor 1 included McDougall,
Jung, Brentano, Adler, Piaget, Fechner, Janet, and Hall. The
theorists with very low scores (or high negative scores if we express
them as sigma scores) include Estes, Watson, Pavlov, Spence, Skinner, Miller, Hull, Guthrie, and Harlow.

At the positive pole of this factor, we find variables that tend to involve an emphasis on conscious processes, content, or intention—on the whole a pattern we might characterize as subjectivistic, mentalistic, phenomenological, or psychological. The negative pole might be described as objectivistic, positivistic, materialistic, or behavioral. I would label this *subjectivistic vs. objectivistic.* The scores of the theorists appear to be consistent with this interpretation.

FACTOR 2

Positive variables:
14. Total organization (.96, .91)
28. Holism (.95, .94)
15. Uniqueness of individual (.65, .75)
21. Naturalistic observation (.55, .68)
 5. Observable behavior (.54, −.25)
10. Social determinants (.42, .43)
24. Finalism (.36, .80)

Negative variables:
27. Elementarism (−.95, −94)
12. Influence of past experience (−.65, −.26)
23. Determinism (−51, −.66)
25. Mechanism (−46, −.76)
29. Nomothetic (−.28, −36)

The high-scoring theorists include Goldstein, Köhler, Koffka, McDougall, Allport, Wertheimer, Lewin, and Rogers. The low-scoring theorists are Spence, Titchener, Estes, Ebbinghaus, Hull, Wundt, Pavlov, and Skinner. The pattern at the positive pole might be characterized as holistic, totalistic, or molar, while that at the negative pole might be called elementaristic, atomistic, or molecular. I would call this factor *holistic vs. elementaristic.*

At this point, the factors already cast an interesting light on some of the speculative analyses of theoretical orientation that I noted. Factors 1 and 2 seem to correspond to the two basic dimensions described by Brunswik and support his contention that these dimensions correspond to logically separable issues. It so happens, however, that there is a substantial positive correlation between the two factors. Thus, in the sample of theorists who were rated, subjectivism tends to go with holism and objectivism tends to go with elementarism. Within the sample, we can find a few exceptions to the rule, but the correlation is nonetheless consistent with Allport's

Lockean-Leibnitzean dichotomy and with similar unidimensional treatments. But let us note that there are still other dimensions to consider, and neither Allport nor Brunswik has done them full justice.

FACTOR 3

Positive variables:
29. Nomothetic (.89, .69)
34. Physical analogies (.87, .76)
13. Immediate external determinants (.69, .83)
 2. Sensation and perception (.62, .43)
33. Hypothetical entities (.60, .01)
18. Rigidly controlled experimentation (.50, .75)
1. Learning (.31, .36)

Negative variables:
16. Persisting traits (−.66, −.84)
15. Uniqueness of individual (−.57, −.76)
30. Normative generalization (−.40, −.19)
10. Social determinants (−.29, −.44)
 7. Emotion (−.26, −.50)
 6. Unconscious processes (−.21, −.65)

High-scoring theorists include Koffka, Köhler, Hull, Estes, Wertheimer, Skinner, Lashley, Titchener, and Müller. Low-scoring theorists include Rorschach, Binet, Adler, Jung, Terman, Janet, Allport, Charcot, and Hall. The nomothetic outlook is common to all the positive variables in the sense that they all tend to stress processes, structures, or experience as such rather than the behaving or experiencing individual. Variables at the negative pole are more concerned with characteristics of individuals, though not necessarily in the sense of an idiographic approach. There is a tendency for high-scoring theorists to be experimentalists and for low-scoring theorists to be clinicians. At the core of the factor, however, is an opposition between theory that focuses on processes or structures more or less independently of the people who exhibit them and theory that is concerned with characteristics that can be used to describe individual people. I originally called this factor transpersonal vs. personal, but the former term has since come into wide usage with a meaning much different from the one I had in mind. To avoid unnecessary confusion, I would now call this *apersonal vs. personal.*

FACTOR 4

Positive variables:
19. Statistical analysis (1.05, .95)
32. Quantitative description (.88, .97)
31. Quantitative formulation (.79, .93)
30. Normative generalization (.76, .75)
18. Rigidly controlled experimentation (.48, .75)
26. Operational definition (.47, .71)
 5. Observable behavior (.44, .55)
11. Heredity (.41, .16)
29. Nomothetic (.26, .35)

Negative variables:
 7. Emotion (−.48, −.54)
 6. Unconscious processes (−.29, −.60)
20. "Armchair" speculation (−.28, −.73)
12. Influence of past experience (−.23, −.01)
23. Determinism (−.23, .38)
17. Introspective report (−.18, −.54)

High-scoring theorists include Estes, Thurstone, Spearman, Terman, Spence, Binet, Ebbinghaus, and Miller, while the low-scoring theorists include Freud, Janet, Goldstein, Charcot, Jung, Wertheimer, Sullivan, Köhler, and Koffka. The four most prominent variables are all concerned with quantification. Accompanying them at the positive pole are variables concerned with methodological precision. The negative pole is less clearly marked, but the variables suggest content and procedures that do not readily permit quantitative treatment. The high-scoring theorists are all concerned with either quantitative measurement or mathematical formulation, while the low-scoring theorists are not concerned with either of these. I call this *quantitative vs. qualitative*. The label, like the factor itself, is more clearly definable at the positive pole than at the negative.

FACTOR 5

Positive variables:
 3. Motivation (.98, .94)
12. Influence of past experience (.80, .67)
33. Hypothetical entities (.73, .47)
 1. Learning (.57, .42)

10. Social determinants (.55, .73)
 7. Emotion (.49, .67)
29. Nomothetic (.38, −.14)
 6. Unconscious processes (.38, .45)
 8. Self-concept (.39, .51)
24. Finalism (.32, .34)
16. Persisting traits (.22, .52)

Negative variables:
 2. Sensation and perception (−.32, −.59)
17. Introspective reports (−.14, −.22)
32. Quantitative description (−.16, −.38)
30. Normative generalization (−.15, −.23)

High scorers include McDougall, Jung, Adler, Mowrer, Sullivan, Freud, and James. Low-scoring theorists include Titchener, Wundt, Mach, Fechner, Wertheimer, Ebbinghaus, Spearman, and Külpe. There is a varied assortment of content variables at the positive pole, but in contrast to those at the negative pole, they all show a concern with processes or change. The negative pole is not as well marked, but it does seem to involve content that might be considered static or structural and methods that might be used to isolate features of this content. I would label this *dynamic vs. static,* though these terms are a little too value laden and the factor itself is probably the least well defined of the set.

FACTOR 6

Positive variables:
 9. Biological determinants (.80, .59)
11. Heredity (.78, .75)
34. Physical analogies (.40, .10)
21. Naturalistic observation (.38, .56)

Negative variables:
10. Social determinants (−.39, −.14)
 1. Learning (−.21, −.35)
 8. Self-concept (−.16, .19)
26. Operational definition (−.17, −.42)
13. Immediate external determinants (−.16, −.40)

The most conspicuous positive theorists are Galton, Freud, Jung, Hall, McDougall, and Cannon. The negative theorists are Skinner,

Titchener, Ebbinghaus, Angell, Hull, Rogers, and Watson. In this case, the overall character of the polarity is obvious. There is a biological emphasis at the positive pole and an emphasis on social determinants and learning at the negative pole. The nature-nurture issue is clearly tied to this factor, but I do not see this as the essence of the factor. To be sure, a constitutional emphasis goes with the positive pole and an environmental emphasis with the negative pole, but scoring at either end of the continuum seems to be dependent essentially on focusing primary attention on one set of determinants, rather than on a position on the nature-nature issue. It seems to me, then, that the factor basically contrasts an orientation toward internal sources of behavior as opposed to external sources. My label for this is *endogenist vs. exogenist.*

Since this is an oblique solution, the six factors are intercorrelated to some degree, and it is possible to apply factor analysis once again to the interfactor correlations. Such an analysis was performed, and it yielded two factors which were rotated to the best approximation to simple structure. This kind of analysis—known generally as second-order or second-stratum analysis—yields factors broader in scope than the original (first-order) factors, but strictly speaking, these second-order factors cannot contain any new content. They can only represent trends that are common to the first-order factors from which they are derived, just as the first-order factors can only represent trends common to the variables with which we started.

The first of the second-order factors, factor A, has the following loadings on the six first-order factors: .82, .75, .00, −.88, −.14, .14. Thus, it is related to factors 1 and 2 in a positive way and to factor 4 in a negative way. At its positive pole it expresses whatever is common to those orientations I have called subjectivistic, holistic, and qualitative, while at its negative pole it expresses qualities I have characterized as objectivistic, elementaristic, and quantitative. There can be no doubt that this corresponds to the Leibnitzean-Lockean dichotomy described by Allport and to a variety of parallel dichotomies described by other writers. It is difficult to find a pair of terms that captures all the ingredients of this broad dimension, but I have called it *synthetic vs. analytic.*

Factor B displays the following set of loadings: −.10, .13, −.72, .00, .64, .36. It bears a strong positive relationship to factor 5, a strong negative relationship to factor 3, and a weak or moderate positive relationship to factor 6. Thus, it contrasts an orientation that is personal, dynamic, and somewhat endogenist with an orientation that is apersonal, static, and somewhat exogenist. The overall pattern is reminiscent of the clash between James and some of the experimentalists of his day. Indeed, if we were to derive scores for this second-order factor, James would be quite high (though Jung would probably be the highest) and Titchener would probably score lowest. I think this factor can be roughly characterized as *functional vs. structural*.

This does not quite complete the analysis, for there is a positive correlation (.55) between factor A and factor B. It is thus possible to recognize a still broader dimension common to both of them. This would in fact be a general factor common to the entire domain we are considering. But it must be noted that while this factor is general and thus exerts a pervasive influence, affecting nearly all the variables studied, its influence is a weak one. We could describe theorists in terms of their standings on the general factor, but we could describe them with far greater precision in terms of their standings on the six first-order factors. What is this general factor? It is obviously synthetic and functional at the positive pole and analytic and structural at the negative pole. To relate it to first-order factors, we could say that it contrasts an orientation that is subjectivistic, holistic, qualitative, personal, dynamic, and endogenist with an orientation that is objectivistic, elementaristic, quantitative, apersonal, static, and exogenist. The former orientation suggests an inclination to experience people and life in all their complexity, while the latter suggests a tendency to deal with reality in a more controlling, analytical, compartmental way, restricting attention and isolating entities and events from the total context. I have characterized this opposition as *fluid vs. restrictive,* although no available terms are entirely satisfactory. James, McDougall, and Jung appear to be fairly good examples of the fluid orientation while Skinner, Ebbinghaus, and Estes evidently represent the restrictive pole.

All the essential relationships I have noted here among the factors and between the factors and the original variables are represented in diagrammatic form in Figure 1. The original variables are presented in the middle of the diagram. As we proceed outward to either the left or the right, we can see the relationships between these variables and the more general trends represented by the first-order factors, then the second-order factors, and finally the general dimension of fluid vs. restrictive orientation. Obviously I have discarded a great deal of numerical information here for the sake of simplicity. I have drawn connecting lines to represent only the most substantial loadings. Thus, the groupings represented by the converging lines in this double hierarchy point to patterns of variables that are frequently found together. Other, less common patterns are still possible. Perhaps we should bear in mind that life itself is far more complicated than anything we can say about it. This sort of diagram can give us a rough picture of the shape of thought in a science. Rough and simple as it is, I trust it is a bit richer than most of the published attempts to describe in a global way the basic patterns of orientation in psychology.

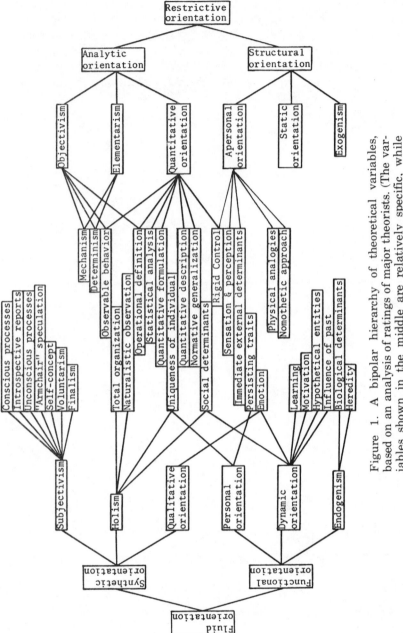

Figure 1. A bipolar hierarchy of theoretical variables, based on an analysis of ratings of major theorists. (The variables shown in the middle are relatively specific, while those on the left and right sides represent more general and mutually opposing trends.)

3. The Development of Theoretical Orientation Survey

THE ANALYSIS OF SELF-REPORT DATA

After isolating dimensions of theoretical orientation that underlie differences among widely recognized theorists, I decided to examine patterns of orientation in a somewhat different population with a different measurement medium—to study the self-reported views and positions of contemporary psychologists in general. At this point, I could have simply assumed that I had isolated *the* basic dimensions underlying theoretical orientation in psychology and proceeded to develop questionnaire scales to measure them. For a number of reasons, I felt this would be a mistake. While we may be dealing with the same domain of variables in both cases—the domain of theoretical orientation—the discriminations that are possible vary with the medium. Hence, it may be possible by analyzing data yielded by one mode of measurement to isolate certain dimensions that could not be found at all if we started with data yielded by a different mode of measurement. Rating data and questionnaire data yield somewhat different kinds of information. When we rate another person, we can do so only in terms of what he outwardly expresses or in terms of what we imagine or project. We can respond to questionnaire items, on the other hand, in terms of a host of dispositions that may not be apparent to others who observe us. There is a difference in both overtness of expression and in specificity. We can direct questionnaire items to very specific issues on which it would not be possible to obtain meaningful ratings for a group of theorists. The individual respondent will know how he himself stands on the issue, but he cannot tell from their writings how Freud, Jung, Rogers, Skinner, and Wundt stand on it.

Thus, the measurement medium makes a difference. The target population does also. The major theorists spanned almost a century of psychology, and an issue on which the climate of opinion has undergone great changes could yield conspicuous individual differences. Conceivably the variance on such an issue could shrink to zero in a contemporary sample of psychologists. Obviously in gathering questionnaire data I could utilize only contemporary samples. The shift from major theorists to a more representative group also makes an important difference. An issue that seems vital to people who are actively engaged in formulating theory may seem unimportant to those who are not involved in such pursuits. Thus, the issue of formal vs. informal theory is likely to concern people who construct theory, and this issue assumed particular prominence in the 1940s. There are many facets of this issue, however, that may seem inconsequential to most people whose careers are devoted to the practical application of psychology. For them, there may be other issues, of minor interest to the theorists, that assume great importance.

Perhaps we should also note that rating major theorists is not quite the same thing as rating other psychologists whom we know from first-hand acquaintance. The theorist is known to us from the psychological literature we have read, and this literature is likely to contain an abundance of secondary sources. Thus, we come to know about Wundt, Titchener, and James through the packaged presentations of modern textbooks on history and systems. These textbooks contain contemporary biases. They contain frameworks and perspectives that differ from those of books published in 1900. If these contemporary presentations do not predetermine the dimensions that can be extracted from theorist ratings, they nonetheless add bits of distortion to the ratings of particular theorists on particular variables. Presumably an analysis of self-report data should yield results totally free of this kind of bias.

In 1969, I began constructing items for questionnaire research. As in the earlier research I sought initially to cover the domain of theoretical orientation, capturing in items all important issues on which positions varied. The variables used in the rating research and the factors derived from them served as one guide to item construction, but I consulted many sources for further ideas. The result was a collection of items that covered many different topics. There were items relating to many forms of content bias, to a variety of methodological issues, to modes of conceptualization, to criteria for evaluating theory, and to views on the ideal personality. There were items covering many possible basic assumptions regarding the nature of the mind, regarding human nature, regarding the nature of causality, regarding the kinds of principles that underlie human behavior, and regarding the relationship of mental and behavioral events to physiological events. Some items called for opinions, while others called for an expression of personal attitudes or values.

To the extent that it was possible, the initial pool of items probably provided comprehensive coverage. There are limits to what can be covered in a set of items designed to meet all the essential requirements for productive use. It was essential for one thing to have items that would actually discriminate. An ideal item would yield approximately equal numbers of *agree* and *disagree* answers, while an item for which all answers were identical would be useless for measurement purposes. This means that for some issues that seem important in principle no usable items can be constructed. Perhaps the body-mind problem best illustrates the point. There are a number of possible positions on this issue, but only a position that is espoused by a large number of psychologists and at the same time rejected by a large number provides the basis for a usable item. Some theoretically possible positions do not qualify. It is likely that most psychologists today do not even have well-defined positions on the issue. Fundamental as the issue is to psychological theory, it is rarely treated as a focal issue by most psychologists. They tend for the most part to ignore the issue, but to accept formally a position advocated by their teachers—most likely, some sort of double-aspect view—but move informally to alternative positions when they proceed to more specific psychological issues. Since the body-mind issue per se is not focal, they do not worry too much about the conflict. Thus, I discovered early that psychologists will overwhelming reject a statement to the effect that "the body and the mind should be regarded as independent entities." Just as overwhelmingly, however, they endorse the idea that "bodily processes can be influenced extensively by mental processes." The body-mind issue is complex and subtle, but most psychologists do not address themselves to its intricacies, and it is my guess that the individual differences in their views could be largely represented in terms of a single dimension of subjectivism-objectivism.

There were additional requirements that satisfactory items had to meet. The items had to cover a very broad domain but with reasonable economy (since I could not expect psychologists to take questionnaires containing hundreds of items). This meant that the individual items had to be fairly broad and general in scope and were likely to be formulated in more abstract terms than the items typically used in attitude and personality inventories. It seemed desirable at the same time to phrase the items in such a way that they would continue to be usable for a long period of time. Thus, it was necessary to avoid both terminology and issues that were too narrowly current. Furthermore, it was important to have items that could be understood by psychologists in all fields. They had to be free of specialized vocabulary.

It is important in all questionnaire work, of course, to strive for items that are free of vagueness and ambiguity. This proved particularly difficult in the present research, for this requirement was not fully compatible with the other requirements. Almost any statement one can make about a general psychological issue, expressed in the common vocabulary and not in technical jargon, is bound to sound vague or ambiguous to someone. One can merely hope to reduce vagueness without at the same time making item content too narrow. At this point, I can only hope I have achieved a balance that most psychologists will find tolerable. Actually, there is a bit more to this matter than an incompatibility between generality and clarity. The vocabulary we employ is dependent on the positions we take on certain basic issues, and the differences in viewpoint are such that certain words that seem essential for expressing one viewpoint may be considered meaningless by those who hold a different viewpoint. Thus, it seems in the nature of the present material that a certain level of unclarity is inevitable.

Before assembling the questionnaire that I would subject to factor analysis, I subjected items to preliminary testing. I sent each of two sets of items to several dozen psychologists. I asked each correspondent first to respond to all items in terms of a five-point Likert scale, that contained the categories *strongly agree, agree, uncertain, disagree,* and *strongly disagree,* and then to write any comments or criticisms regarding the items that seemed appropriate. Particular items that seemed deficient were to be indicated. From response tallies, I identified the items that yielded an overabundance on either the *agree* or the *disagree* side and, if possible, modified them in such a way as to achieve better discrimination. I also revised items that yielded a large number of *uncertain* responses and items that were regarded by correspondents as vague, ambiguous, double-barreled, or weak in some other respect. From the revised items, I assembled the first Theoretical Orientation Survey [TOS(I)].

THE ANALYSIS OF THEORETICAL ORIENTATION SURVEY (I)

TOS(I) contained 120 theoretical orientation items and 25 items in which the subject was asked to indicate the strength of his interest in various areas in psychology. In 1970, the questionnaire, an answer sheet, and a return envelope were sent to each of several hundred psychologists. Provided they were willing to complete the questionnaire, correspondents were asked to return the answer sheet. In this mailing, in the earlier item testing, and in all subsequent stages of the questionnaire research, I took names in sequence from the most recent APA Directory listing. At each stage of the research that called for a fresh mailing, I began the selection at the point where I had previously ended it in the alphabetical listing. This procedure obviously does not ensure a random sample of APA members, much less of psychologists at large, but it does ensure that no name will be duplicated in successive mailings. Any sampling bias introduced by this procedure is certainly inconsequential compared to the unavoidable bias created by the subsequent self-selection imposed by the recipients of my questionnaire forms. On the whole, the return rate for my questionnaires has run between 30 and 35 percent. In view of the amount of labor I have requested from busy professional people, this seems a fairly satisfactory rate.

It was only in the later stages of data collection that I actually sought a sample representative of psychologists in general. In the rating research, I had wanted a rather specialized group of correspondents. In the course of developing the Theoretical Orientation Survey, I thought it best to seek correspondents who would have a relatively high level of interest in theoretical issues. I assumed that on the whole, people in academic positions would have a greater investment in these issues than would people in the nonacademic world. Therefore, instead of taking all names as I proceeded through the APA Directory, I initially took only people in identifiably academic positions. Once the Theoretical Orientation Survey was constructed in final form and I began to seek normative data, however, I proceeded to take all names in sequence without regard to employment status. The decision of the individual psychologist to participate or not participate remains a factor in all the sampling. There is no definitive way of assessing the differences between participants and nonparticipants, but there are some bits of pertinent data that we will consider later in this chapter.

Completed answer sheets for TOS(I) were returned by 298 subjects. Principal-axis factor analysis was applied to the intercorrelations of the 120 orientation items. Seventeen factors were extracted and rotated to the closest approximation to oblique simple structure. The interest variables were treated as extension variables, so that they could not directly influence the basic character of the factor solution. Their loadings and factor-correlations were derived at a later stage in data processing. We shall consider the findings for the interest variables in a later chapter.

All 17 factors appeared to be interpretable in terms of meaningful facets of theoretical orientation. Perhaps this is not surprising in view of the varied assortment of items that were analyzed. Of course, the factors are not all of equal importance. In the final solution the factors were arranged in order of decreasing variance magnitude, and on the whole the factors near the beginning of the series are the ones that would most fundamentally color a psychologist's outlook. These are also the factors that are best represented in item content, most clearly interpretable, and most likely to prove replicable in later research.

I can best give the reader an overview of the results of this analysis by presenting a brief description of each factor, along with a couple of salient variables (items substantially loaded by the given factor but not too highly loaded by any other factor):

1. *Factual vs. theoretical orientation:* At one pole, we find a radically empirical outlook. At the other pole, there is an emphasis on the value of speculation, interpretation, or theory building.

> *Positive item:* A science is likely to progress most rapidly if researchers devote themselves primarily to the systematic gathering of factual information and engage in little elaborate speculation or theory building.

> *Negative item:* It is just as important for psychological researchers to formulate theoretical interpretations as it is to accumulate specific facts about behavior.

2. *Impersonal causality vs. personal will:* At the positive pole, we find a determinism that excludes or deemphasizes individual choice or participation. The negative pole stresses the importance of individual choice, purpose, and uniqueness.

> *Positive item:* Human behavior is characterized in all aspects by lawful regularity, and thus, in principle, it is completely predictable.

> *Positive item:* Human actions are just as strictly determined by whatever causes are operating as all other physical events are.

3. *Experiential content emphasis vs. behavioral content emphasis:* This is clearly a central ingredient of subjectivism vs. objectivism, but the concern here is essentially with the subject matter deemed appropriate for psychology. Related methodological issues appear elsewhere, for example, in factor 9.

> *Positive item:* The individual subject's personal account of his private conscious experience is one of the most valuable sources of psychological data.

> *Negative item:* In general, concepts of *ego* and *self* serve no essential function, and the science of psychology can do as well without them.

4. *Holism vs. elementarism:* The items loaded by this factor are concerned with this dimension in regard to both research strategy and theory, with the former receiving the greater emphasis.

> *Positive item:* We can best achieve comprehensive understanding

if we concentrate on global patterns and relationships before
proceeding to investigate the more elementary relationships of
component variables.

Negative item: Psychology can best progress as a science if we
concentrate first on elementary mechanisms and relationships
before proceeding to complex problems that involve the total
personality.

5. *Biological determinism:* The loaded content of this factor suggests
something akin to the rating factor of endogenism vs. exogenism.
That polarity, however, is represented in some way by both factor 5
and factor 6 in the present series. The concern in factor 5 is essentially with the importance of genetic factors as determinants of observed characteristics in both the individual and the species.

Positive item: Much of the variation in human temperament is
governed by inborn constitution.

Positive item: Many of the behavioral differences between men
and women are a function of inherent biological differences between the sexes.

6. *Environmental determinism:* The primary emphasis here is on the
social environment as a source of individual differences.

Positive item: It is a mistake to think in terms of a fixed individual constitution, since through appropriate early training, we
could cause a normal infant to develop almost any kind of personality.

Positive item: Individual differences in personality are mostly a
product of environmental influence.

7. *Humanism vs. scientific detachment:* The positive role combines a
variety of features that might be called humanistic, e.g., a belief in
the goodness of human nature, a concern with the needs of people,
and an advocacy of intensive study of individuals. At the negative
pole, we find, along with detachment, a tendency in theory to deal
with human behavior in the same manner as with other kinds of
physical events.

Positive item: If there is minimal interference with the development of their natural tendencies, people will behave in a way
that is predominantly benevolent and cooperative.

Positive item: Psychologists could learn more if they devoted
more time to the intensive study of a few individuals and less
time to large-scale research with restricted features of behavior.

8. *Emphasis on phylogenetic continuity vs. emphasis on human distinctiveness:* The positive pole stresses cross-species equivalence,
while the negative pole stresses the emergent character of human
choice and purpose.

Positive item: Human behavior should be studied by methods

that are logically identical with those we employ in studying lower animals. It requires no fundamentally different procedure.
Negative item: Adequate explanation of human behavior requires principles that are not needed to explain the behavior of lower animals.

9. *Physicalism:* This appears to capture a methodological component of objectivism in the sense that the positive pole emphasizes physicalistic reduction, or explanation in terms of physical conditions and events. Alternatively, we might construe the primary emphasis as one of stimulus determinism, since the specific focus stressed in explanation is on antecedent and contemporaneous stimuli, but stimulus determinism appears to be more the direct concern of factor 2. The negative pole would logically involve subjectivistic explanation and antireductionism, but it is not well marked by available items.

Positive item: The primary goal of psychological theory should be laws in which behavior is expressed as a complex function of present and past stimulation.

Positive item: In scientific writing, psychologists should either avoid making statements about conscious phenomena or try to translate such statements into statements about physical conditions and events.

10. *Emphasis on unconscious motivation vs. emphasis on conscious motivation:* This factor is mainly concerned with whether people are or are not aware of the primary sources of their actions. The latter could be called *irrationalism,* but *rationalism* would be a misleading label for the negative pole.

Positive item: Most of our behavior is governed by forces of which we are unaware.

Negative item: People are usually aware of the most important motives or reasons underlying their actions.

11. *Systematism:* This title is suggested by the two best-loaded items. At the positive pole, the major emphasis is on systematic hypothesis testing, but there is an accompanying emphasis on theory construction. This pole is suggestive of hypothetico-deductive method. The negative pole is poorly marked but seems to entail an anticonstructionist attitude.

Positive item: In research, one should nearly always start with a clear-cut hypothesis that can be evaluated statistically.

Positive item: Most of our research should be devoted to the testing of hypotheses clearly derived from systematically formulated theory.

12. *Quantitative vs. qualitative orientation:* This appears to be the

equivalent of the rating factor so designated. As in the earlier research, the former pole is better defined than the latter and is accompanied by a general favoring of systematic research methodology.

Positive item: Psychological theory could benefit greatly from more extensive use of mathematical and geometric models.

Positive item: As this science progresses, psychological theories will tend increasingly to be composed of abstract mathematical or logical equations.

13. *Physiological reductionism:* Both factor 13 and factor 14 involve an emphasis on physiological processes. Here the stress seems to be on the ultimate explanatory power of physiological variables.

Positive item: The most useful type of explanation for most behavioral or psychological phenomena would be in terms of physiological processes or mechanisms.

Positive item: Probably the most fruitful way of accounting for dream phenomena is in terms of physiological processes.

14. *Emphasis on physiological correlates:* There are two well-loaded items that involve psychophysiological covariation, but these are accompanied by items that emphasize individual expression. The combination looks a bit accidental; this is probably not a replicable factor.

Positive item: Every event in conscious experience is accompanied by a parallel physiological process that undergoes change whenever the conscious event changes.

Positive item: Eventually a neurological or biochemical correlate will be found for every important feature of behavior and experience.

15. *Rejection vs. advocacy of physical theoretical models:* This is also a factor of insubstantial variance. The title is suggested by the three best-loaded items.

Positive item: Psychologists should avoid incorporating physical models into psychological theory and treating psychological systems as analogous to mechanical, hydraulic, or electrical systems.

Negative items: In explaining psychological processes, it is often useful to describe them in terms of a physical analogy, i.e., in terms of a physical process that has similar properties.

16. *Explicit conceptualization:* This label fits the one well-loaded item. The content of the other loaded items does not conflict with this, but it does not display a very coherent pattern.

Positive item: At every stage in the development of his thinking about an area, a theorist should try to express his ideas in the form of an explicit system of concepts and propositions. Theory is not just an ultimate goal.

Positive item: All aspects of conscious human experience should be considered appropriate subject matter for psychology.

17. *Psychophysical dualism:* Here again we have a loose assortment of poorly loaded items. The label is based on the content of the best-loaded item.

Positive item: Body and mind should be regarded as somewhat different things rather than merely different aspects of the same thing.

Positive item: By nature, human beings tend to be more aggressive than the members of many other species.

Five second-order factors were derived from the intercorrelations among these first-order factors and rotated to a position of oblique simple structure. The rotated factors were identified as follows:

I. *Objectivism vs. subjectivism:* This has very high positive loadings for factors 1, 8, and 9 are high negative loadings for factors 3 and 4.

II. *Exogenism vs. endogenism:* This loads factor 6 positively and factor 5 negatively.

III. *Natural science orientation:* Here substantial positive loadings for factors 13 and 14 are accompanied by a negative loading for factor 15.

IV. *Formalism:* Here the highest loadings, both positive, are for factors 11 and 16.

V. *Personal vs. apersonal orientation:* The most substantial loading is for factor 17, followed by a modest loading for factor 7.

The total loading pattern was taken into account in the interpretation of each factor, and these designations all appear to be well supported. The first two of these factors are of much greater significance than the other three because together they possess all the high loadings for the large variance factors in the first half of the first-order series. Factors III, IV, and V make psychological sense, but they rest more heavily on weak first-order factors that are less likely to reappear in future studies.

It is possible to extract one general factor at the third-order level from the intercorrelations among the second-order factors. It loads factor III most highly and factors I and IV more modestly. Its loadings for factors II and V are rather weak. The relationships among factors at the three successive strata are shown in the form of bipolar hierarchy in Figure 2. This diagram highlights some of

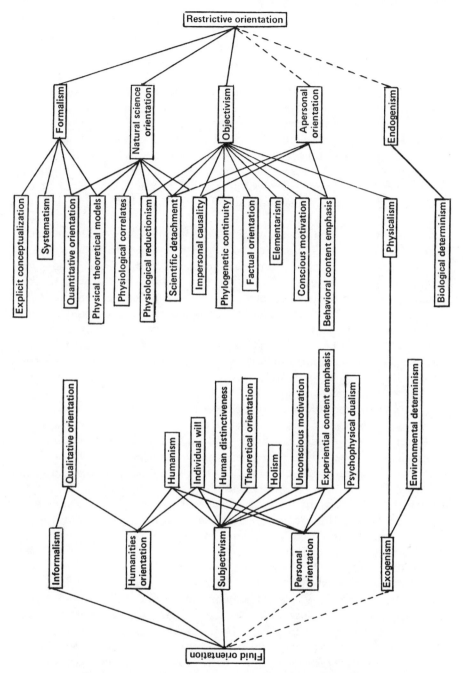

Figure 2. A bipolar hierarchy of theoretical-orientation factors, based on an analysis of questionnaire data. (The first-order factors are shown in the middle. On either side are terms representing the two poles of each second-order factor. The terms at the extreme left and right represent the third-order polarity. Prominent loadings are represented by connecting lines.)

the differences between the present analysis and the earlier analysis of rating data.

Some differences between the two analyses were definitely expected. Since the questionnaire items were more numerous than the rating variables and more specific in content, they were expected to yield a greater number of factors and factors of greater specificity of content. This expectation was certainly met, and we may note that there is an overall tendency for the questionnaire analysis to yield first-order factors that correspond to some of the original variables in the rating study and second-order factors that correspond to first-order rating factors.

Some departures from this general rule and some shifts in focus from the one factor system to the other follow naturally from basic differences between the two measurement media. Since the two measurement techniques do not lend themselves equally well to the same areas of content, there are unavoidable differences in the density with which various areas are sampled and represented in the initial pool of variables. In spite of such differences, however, it can be said that all the rating factors appear in some recognizable form among the questionnaire factors. Perhaps the greatest difference between the two systems simply lies in the fact that the questionnaire factors contain some additional, novel content.

Lest I be accused of exaggerating the similarities between the two solutions, let me also call attention to the fact that the use of the same label to designate both a rating factor and a questionnaire may obscure subtle differences between the two factors so labeled. It was not my intention to obscure the differences, because in each case I chose the available term that seemed most appropriate. The differences are mostly in the level of referent generality of factors.[1] For example, the rating factor designated *quantitative vs. qualitative orientation* is probably a bit broader in scope than the corresponding questionnaire factor. It may represent something intermediate between that factor and the second-order factor of *formalism*.

In the rating study, *subjectivism vs. objectivism* and *holism vs. elementarism* appeared as independent but correlated factors at the first-order level. Because of differences in sampling patterns for the two media, the questionnaire analysis yields a holism factor at the first-order level, but subjectivism is multiply represented there. *Subjectivism vs. objectivism* appears as a factor at the second-order level, although at that level it is actually broader than the factor of the same name in the earlier research. Indeed, it encompasses *holism vs. elementarism* as one of its loaded ingredients—making it more comparable in scope to the general factor of *fluid vs. restrictive orientation.* Indeed, if we discard the small-variance questionnaire factors (and the second-order factors that they generate), *subjectivism vs. objectivism* comes close to being *the* general factor in the questionnaire analysis.

The factor of *exogenism vs. endogenism* appears in both studies, but its associations with other factors in either study appear to be the reverse of what they are in the other study. Thus, in the rating study, endogenism went with the general pattern of fluid orientation, while exogenism went with the general pattern of restrictive orientation. In the questionnaire study, we see the opposite pattern. In actuality, the shift is a minor one, since *exogenism vs. endogenism* proves to be a fairly independent factor statistically in each study and is only weakly loaded by higher-order factors in both sets of data.

THE ANALYSIS OF THEORETICAL ORIENTATION SURVEY (II)

The analysis of TOS(I) was undertaken in part simply to illuminate the dimensions of theoretical orientation that could be discerned in self-report data, but it also served as a foundation for the development of scales that could be employed in many subsequent studies. It seemed most practical and fruitful to concentrate efforts at scale development on those questionnaire factors of large variance that had clear and meaningful loading patterns. The factors chosen for this purpose were the first six of the above series and factors 9 and 12—in other words, *factual vs. theoretical orientation, impersonal causality vs. personal will, experiential content emphasis vs. behavioral content emphasis, holism vs. elementarism, biological determinism, environmental determinism, physicalism,* and *quantitative vs. qualitative orientation.* It was assumed that scales for these factors would afford a basis as well for assessing subjects on the second-order factors of *objectivism vs. subjectivism* and *exogenism vs. endogenism.*

For each of the eight target factors, well-loaded items were selected from TOS(I). Many additional items of content that appeared appropriate for any of these factors were constructed. Once again, a set of items was sent to an APA sample for testing, and items were revised in such a way as to increase discriminatory power and to reduce various weakness. The revised items were combined with the items selected from TOS(I) to form a second Theoretical Orientation Survey, which I shall designate TOS(II). TOS(II) contained altogether 103 prospective scale items. In addition, it contained two items designed to assess attitudes toward the research:

It is worthwhile to study the theoretical orientations of psychologists.
On the whole, the items in this questionnaire are well-designed.

These appeared as items 104 and 105, and it was hoped that they might provide some clues regarding differences between respondents and nonrespondents to the questionnaire (on the assumption that nonrespondents would tend to resemble the respondents who disagreed with these two items). In items 106 through 125, the subject was asked to indicate the extent to which he agreed or disagreed with the views of each of 20 theorists. Finally, at the end of the questionnaire, the subject was asked to indicate the one theorist in the list whose views were closest to his own.

TOS(II) was mailed to about 1000 APA members. Answer sheets were completed and returned by 341 individuals and subjected to analysis. Principal-axis extraction was applied to the 103 theoretical-orientation items, and the remaining items were treated as extension variables. As expected, TOS(II) yielded fewer factors than TOS(I). The number of factors that merited rotation, however, was not altogether clear, and two rotational solutions were obtained independently—one based on the first nine extracted factors, the other based on 13 factors. In each case, the factors were rotated blindly to the best approximation to oblique simple structure.

Examination of item-factor correlations and factor loadings revealed that in each solution there were eight factors that corresponded clearly to the eight target factors, both in terms of the pattern shown for new items and in terms of the pattern for items transferred from TOS(I). There was a close correspondence between the two solutions with respect to seven of the factors. The exception was the factor of *physicalism*. Though this factor was identifiable in both solutions, it loaded a few items in each solution that it failed to load significantly in the other solution. The "surplus" factors—of which there was one in the nine-factor solution and there were five in the thirteen-factor solution—were all of small variance and lacked clear loading patterns. They did not appear to warrant interpretation.

Both rotational solutions yielded two second-order factors. With respect to their loadings on and correlations with the eight target factors, the second-order factors display a very close correspondence from one solution to the other. In each solution, there is a factor of *objectivism vs. subjectivism,* which displays large positive loadings for *impersonal causality, physicalism,* and *quantitative orientation,* a weak positive loading on *factual orientation,* and large negative loadings on *experiential content emphasis* and *holism.* As a consequence of a change in the total factor context, we can see some shift in emphasis here from the pattern of the *objectivism vs. subjectivism* factor derived from TOS(I), but there can be no question that we are dealing with essentially the same dimension. The other second-order factor in each solution is unmistakably *endogenism vs. exogenism.* In each case, it has two large loadings, a positive one for *biological determinism* and a negative one for *environmental determinism.* In both solutions, there is a moderate negative correlation between the two second-order factors ($-.46$ in the nine-factor solution and $-.24$ in the thirteen-factor solution). From the relationship found in the TOS(I) analysis between these factors and the fluid-restrictive polarity, we might have expected a positive correlation, with objectivism going with exogenism. In the TOS(I) analysis, however, these two second-order factors actually correlated essentially zero ($-.02$). We may note that in the present analysis, the restrictive-fluid polarity is really best represented by the factor of *objectivism vs. subjectivism* alone, rather than by a third-stratum combination of this with the other factor.

Factor loadings and correlations were obtained for items 104 to 125 by the Dwyer extension method. I shall consider only the item-factor correlations, since they are more directly interpretable. For the eight target factors, these correlations prove to be virtually identical for the nine-factor and thirteen-factor solutions—in most cases they differ by no more than two points in the second decimal place. Hence, we can make essentially the same general observations from examining either set of data. Item 104 yields only two correlations greater than .20—for the first and third factors. According to these correlations, those who consider it worthwhile to study the theoretical orientations of psychologists tend to be theoretically oriented ($r = -.22$ and $-.21$) and tend toward an emphasis on experiential content ($r = .27$ and $.29$). To this extent, they share the biases of the psychologist who launched this research. To the extent that factually and behaviorally oriented psychologists deem this sort of investigation less valuable, they may be less likely to participate and may be underrepresented in my samples. It is obvious, of course, that the potential subjects who are most likely to find my questionnaire items interesting at first glance are people with strong interests in theoretical issues. Those who lack such interest are likely to find the questionnaire more tedious and more difficult to complete.

As I expected from the reactions which my work had already evoked, the responses to item 105 ("On the whole, the items in this questionnaire are well-designed.") were well distributed from *strongly agree* to *strongly disagree.* I felt that this question, too, might tap attitudes that would predispose an individual to complete or not complete the questionnaire. If so, these attitudes appear unlikely to bias self-selection sampling in any systematic way, since the item shows little correlation with any of the factors.

In items 106 to 125 I had presented a list of theorists that I hoped would illuminate the factors still further. They are not the 20 most important theorists of all time, but they are fairly well known and they represent a variety of distinctive positions. The list includes most of the theorists who currently enjoy a high level of popularity. The names include Alfred Adler, Gordon W. Allport, Albert Bandura, Raymond B. Cattell, Erik Erikson, Sigmund Freud, Clark Hull, William James, Carl G. Jung, Wolfgang Köhler, Kurt Lewin, Abraham Maslow, Rollo May, William McDougall, Carl R. Rogers, B. F. Skinner, Louis L. Thurstone, Edward C. Tolman, John B. Watson, and Max Wertheimer. For these items the subject used the same Likert scale employed for all preceding items to indicate the extent to which his views agreed or disagreed with those of each theorist.

These theorists evidently do represent positions that are closely tied to the dimensions of theoretical orientation, for most of the correlations between factors and theorist items proved to be significant. Over half of them exceed .25, though the highest is only .59 (between Watson and *physicalism*). Inspection of the total set of correlations reveals a very consistent pattern of relationships between the factors loaded by *objectivism vs. subjectivism* and two groups of theorists that we can call humanists and behaviorists. The humanists correlate positively with *experiential content emphasis* and *holism* and negatively with *factual orientation, impersonal causality, physicalism,* and *quantitative orientation* (a consistently subjectivistic pattern). The behaviorists show the reverse pattern of correlations. The humanists who fit this total pattern (with all values at least above .20 and more often above .40) include Adler, Allport, Erikson, Jung, Maslow, May, and Rogers. The behaviorists include Hull, Skinner, and Watson (though Hull's correlation with *factual orientation* just barely falls short of .20).

Most of the remaining theorists show parts of one pattern or the other. Köhler, Lewin, and Wertheimer come close to the humanist pattern, but—probably because of their experimental orientation—their correlations with *quantitative orientation* are insignificant. McDougall fits the humanist pattern with respect to *impersonal causality* and *experiential content emphasis,* while James fits it with respect to *experiential content emphasis* and *physicalism,* and Freud fits it with respect to *factual orientation* and *experiential content emphasis*. James and Freud were both multifaceted thinkers who attract admirers of many persuasions, and it is not surprising that they both yield sets of rather low correlations.

Toward the other end of the spectrum, Bandura comes close to fitting the behaviorist pattern, but his correlations with *factual orientation* and *quantitative orientation* are very low. The correlations for Tolman are all quite low, and they barely fit the behaviorist pattern for just two factors—*impersonal causality* and *quantitative orientation*. As one would expect, *quantitative orientation* also correlates positively with Cattell and Thurstone, who otherwise do not conform to the behaviorist pattern.

The other two factors, *biological determinism* and *environmental determinism,* yield few high correlations, though the overall pattern seems meaningful. To consider only the correlations that exceed .20, *biological determinism* correlates positively with Cattell, McDougall, and Thurstone and negatively with Bandura and Watson. *Environmental determinism* correlates positively with Bandura, Hull, Skinner, and Watson and negatively with Wertheimer.

I believe that all the correlations I have noted are in the direction that any student of the history of psychology would predict. Thus, they generally support my factor interpretations. They also suggest that the second-order factor of *objectivism vs. subjectivism* corresponds to the basic polarity wherein contemporary humanists and behaviorists part company.

THE DEVELOPMENT OF FACTORED SCALES

The analysis of TOS(II) served to demonstrate the replicability of eight factors of theoretical orientation (and two second-order factors). It also provided the data necessary for the construction of a set of factor scales. To qualify for inclusion in a factor scale, an item would ideally have a high loading and correlation for a given factor and for none of the other factors. It is usually difficult to find many factor-pure items, but unwanted factor variance can be suppressed or canceled out to some extent by appropriate combinations of items within a scale. Since there were two rotational solutions for TOS(II), it seemed desirable to take both into account and select only those items that showed promise in both solutions. This posed a serious problem only for the *physicalism* factor, which differed considerably from one solution to the other. For this factor, however, it was possible to identify a small set of items that satisfactorily represent the ingredients common to both solutions.

It is also desirable to select items in such a way that the resulting scale contains equal numbers of items that contribute positively and negatively to the scale score. Such a condition ensures that scores are independent of an overall tendency to agree or disagree with items. It is possible to meet this condition to only a limited extent with the present factors. Three of them are essentially unipolar in terms of present data—*biological determinism, environmental determinism,* and *physicalism.* For these three factors, sound negative items might be difficult to construct; at best, they would probably tend to be a bit more cumbersome than the items now loaded positively.

A more important consideration is scale length. Obviously the scales must be long enough to ensure adequate reliability. At the same time, the scales must be short enough to permit convenient wide use of the inventory that contains them. The requirements for group research are a bit different from those of individual measurement. A scale that is too short for accurate individual measurement may still be adequate for research in which we are primarily concerned with the correlations that it yields with other measures. From a brief examination of probable scale items in terms of data from the TOS(II) analysis sample, I reasoned that four-item scales would probably be minimally adequate for most purposes. I also felt that eight- to ten-item scales might be a practical upper limit for further studies in which I would be seeking the cooperation of large samples of psychologists.

I sought eight items for each of the first-order factors. For the *physicalism* factor, there were only seven items that I considered satisfactory. I combined these with eight items for each of the other scales to form a 63-item inventory. In this inventory, I arranged the items from the eight scales in a cyclical order, and I altered the factor sequence in such a way that items of closely related content would not be adjacent in the total inventory.

Within a scale, the items were ordered in such a way that the better items (in terms of loading pattern) would appear early in the inventory. As a result the best four items for each factor all appear among the first 32 items of the inventory, the best five items appear among the first 40 items of the inventory, and so on. Thus, if it is necessary for any purpose to shorten the inventory, one can achieve the best possible set of briefer scales by simply dropping items from the end of the inventory. It is desirable to achieve a balance of positive and negative items whatever the length of the scale. Where there was an otherwise indifferent choice to be made in the sequence of items within a scale, this desideratum was sometimes the determining consideration.

The direction of scoring is another matter to be considered in the total design of the inventory. It will be noted that for most of the factors, the direction is an arbitrary matter. A factor of behavioral vs. experiential content emphasis makes as much sense as a factor of experiential vs. behavioral content emphasis. In a scale designed to measure this, it would not matter which end we chose to make the high end and which the low end. In a factor analysis with blind rotation, either end could correspond to the positive pole. For convenience of comparison, in treating the TOS(II) results, I oriented the factors in both rotated solutions in such a way that they matched the corresponding factors of the TOS(I) analysis. In the case of three factors—*biological determinism, environmental determinism,* and *physicalism*—there are no negative items, and the negative pole of the factor is not as well defined as the positive pole. For these three, it seems more natural (strictly speaking, it is simply more conventional and not really essential) to let high scores correspond to the one well-defined pole. For the other factors, there may be good arguments for reversing directionality. As a matter of fact, in order to simplify the scoring of second-order factors, I decided to reverse two of the factors. If we label the eight basic scales of the final version of the Theoretical Orientation Survey (the only inventory I shall hereafter designate by this title) in terms of the high-scoring end, they now run as follows:

1. Factual (vs. theoretical) orientation
2. Impersonal casuality (vs. personal will)
3. Behavioral (vs. experiential) content emphasis
4. Elementarism (vs. holism)
5. Biological determinism
6. Environmental determinism
7. Physicalism
8. Quantitative (vs. qualitative) orientation

For the sake of simplicity of scoring, I also felt it would be best to score each second-order factor on the basis of the best-loaded first-order factors and to combine those with unit weights. Thus, we can obtain a score for *objectivism vs. subjectivism* by simply taking the sum of the scores (based on any scale length employed) for scales 2, 3, 4, 7, and 8. To score for *endogenism vs. exogenism,* we would subtract the score for factor 6 from the score for factor 5. For normative purposes, I have added a constant of 50 to this difference to ensure that all scores are positive. The 63-item Theoretical Orientation Survey (TOS), more detailed information on scoring, and normative data are presented in the Appendix.

The TOS has been used in extensive research which we will consider in the remaining chapters of this book. In the course of this work, I have derived some reliability coefficients that may throw further light on the respective merits of scales of differing length within the inventory. Alpha coefficients were calculated to assess the internal consistency of the scales. For this purpose, the responses of 866 APA-member subjects were used. The results are shown in Table 1.* For the four-item scales, these values range from .618 to .804. For the two second-order factors, which are scored in terms of combinations of scales, they run still higher. As we proceed to longer scales, the alpha values tend to increase, with only factor 6 manifesting a full-scale value that is lower than the four-item scale value. It should be noted that nearly all of the increments from the 32-item inventory to the 63-item inventory are considerably smaller than we would predict by the Spearman-Brown formula, because this formula assumes that the added items are equivalent to the ones already contained in the scale. In each of the present scales, the initial four items will tend to intercorrelate more highly than the ones that appear later. This is not inevitable, but it tends to follow from the fact that they are better loaded by the common factor. Thus, while we reduce the idiosyncratic influence of any individual item as we increase scale length, we tend simultaneously to lower the average interitem correlation.

If we are to judge the scales in terms of internal consistency, the values in Table 1 would indicate that it is best to use the full inventory if we want accurate individual measurement. It appears, however, that we can do almost as well with a 32-item inventory. Perhaps for many purposes, the four-item scales would be adequate. It should be noted, however, that internal consistency is not particularly important in itself. In traditional treatments of psychological measurement, it has been accorded undue attention. In certain realms of measurement, where we are actually sampling equivalent content-valid items in building a scale, internal consistency is vital, for its defines the upper limit to the validity of the scale. In the construction of both empirical and factor scales, the traditional logic is inapplicable, for one may deliberately combine items in a way that reduces internal consistency for the sake of increasing scale validity. For any given scale length in the TOS, there is an overall tendency for the level of the alpha coefficient to vary with the level of the factor loadings and factor correlations of the component items. (Thus, the factor-2 scale contains better-loaded items than does the factor-4 scale.) To this extent, the alpha coefficients express useful

*Tables will be found beginning on page 167.

information, even if it is not the best information for making decisions about scale lengths.

For an instrument of this kind, retest reliability coefficients
provide more useful information than coefficients based on internal
consistency. Retest coefficients, of course, may reflect genuine trait
fluctuation and change over time. Undoubtedly psychologists do
change their views on basic theoretical issues, sometimes rather
drastically, but I think we generally regard theoretical orientation
as a relatively stable system of traits. Therefore, it is reasonable to
expect any instrument designed to assess this system to manifest
high retest reliability. This would be a necessary precondition for
any long-term prediction we might wish to make with TOS scores.

To assess retest reliability, I mailed additional copies of the TOS
to about 300 APA members who had already completed and returned the inventory to me. The retest forms were mailed about
eight months after the original mailing. While the actual interval
between self-administrations of the two forms was subject to variation from one subject to another, the average interval was undoubtedly close to eight months. Retest reliability coefficients were calculated on the basis of 185 returned forms, and the results are shown
in Table 2.

The retest reliability coefficients on the whole are comparable in
magnitude to the alpha coefficients. The increments that we observe
as we progress from the 32-item inventory to the full inventory are
also comparable to those found for the alpha coefficients. They do
not vary quite as widely as the alpha increments, however, and they
provide more consistent evidence for all scales that we can achieve
more satisfactory measurement with the full inventory than with
any shorter version of it. The retest reliabilities too, however, provide evidence that the 32-item inventory may be sufficiently reliable
for some purposes. Ideally, all the reliability coefficients should be
higher than what we have obtained, but it is difficult to attain
higher values with short scales designed to assess rather broad attitudinal dimensions.

4. Changes in Psychology

THE NATURE OF HISTORICAL CHANGE

It is an obvious fact that psychology has a history and that in the course of that history the climate of opinion in this discipline has undergone a variety of changes. The changes have been described in many ways by many people, and I do not wish to present just one more overview of the history of psychology. On the whole, the methods that have been employed to examine historical change have been rather casual. I should like to consider some ways in which a psychology of psychology might deal more systematically with temporal progressions and then present some bits of evidence from my own research. There are many tasks here that await future investigators.

Actually there have been numerous attempts to assess historical trends in a systematic, empirical way, but the methodology has usually been of a rather elementary sort, involving such things as content tabulations of journal content. There are many forms of historical change that require methods that have never been employed. To see better the nature of the problem, we need to consider the possible kinds of historical change and the ways in which each might be demonstrated or assessed. I have dealt with a parallel problem previously in the context of child personality development.[1] In principle, many of the basic types of change and the manifestations that permit systematic study are essentially the same for these two realms of temporal change.

I should like to consider three general types of change, each of which encompasses a number of more specific possibilities:

1. Changes in level in a given dimension
    a. Shifts in central tendency
    b. Shifts in salience
2. Changes in the scope of the system
    a. Expansion

  b. Restriction
3. Changes in the composition of the system
  a. Replacement
  b. Convergence or integration
  c. Divergence or disintegration
  d. Reorganization

In the first general type of change, the same dimensions, issues, or areas remain in effect over time. We can describe the state of affairs at one moment in the same terms we would use for another moment. The change we observe involves positions along the common dimension. In the simplest case, there is a shift in central tendency; i.e., the position that is most typical or average for one moment or period is higher or lower than it is for another moment. This is the sort of change we are talking about when we say that psychology is becoming more empirical, more holistic, less introspectionistic, etc. If the shifts that we observe over a series of occasions or periods are all in the same direction—either toward ever-higher or ever-lower values—then we can characterize it further as a monotonic progression in central tendency. Any progression in which the direction of change is reversed at any point would be nonmonotonic, and many patterns of nonmonotonic progression are possible. There could be a single reversal point. Then, the progression would be one of increase up to that point and subsequent decrease, or just the opposite pattern. With respect to many issues we might expect cyclical fluctuation, with alternating movements toward opposite extremes.

There are more complex kinds of change involving a single dimension that may not be evidenced in a shift in central tendency. A controversial issue may receive a great deal of attention at one time and then fade into the background. When it is in the background, members of the scientific community may be in apparent agreement on the issue, at least paying lip service to a common position, and feel that there is no point in talking or thinking about the issue since it has been resolved. It is more likely to come to the forefront when it is recognized that there is no common ground. One feels compelled to propound a position because one's opponents have obviously erred and need to be apprised of a more sensible viewpoint. I am suggesting, then, that a dimension or issue will tend to be salient at the same time that there is diversity of opinion. If we could somehow score the members of the scientific community with respect to their positions on the issue, we would probably find that the changing salience of the issue would be reflected not so much in shifts in central tendency along the dimension of measurement as in shifts in variance. The circumstance that underlies an increase in variance is one that people are likely to describe in terms of the existence of opposing trends. On the current scene, the behaviorists and humanists are obviously opposed on a variety of issues, and it is possible that they will stimulate developments in opposite directions along a number of dimensions. The dimension of *experiential vs. behavioral content emphasis* has become quite salient. The issues relating to *impersonal causality vs. personal will* have also been thrust into the forefront, with opposite extreme views being presented by Skinner and the existentialists. It is possible that future syntheses will render these issues less focal.

Changes in scope concern the range of subject matter, methods, and issues with which the participants in a given discipline are concerned. In most sciences, there appears to be a long-term trend of expansion. Repeatedly in the history of science, investigators have turned their attention to territories previously neglected, often ones previously considered outside their domain. As subject matter expands and new methods are introduced, new issues may also arise, and the diverse patterns of orientation within the science may become more complex. To encompass all variations in outlook, we may have to deal with additional dimensions along which views can differ. A movement in the opposite direction—toward restriction of subject matter, reduction of methods, and concern with fewer issues—is also possible, but it is difficult to think of good examples in any science. Perhaps psychology would have been the grand exception to the general rule of expansion if the behaviorist platform had ever been universally adopted, for in its most radical forms behaviorism certainly represents an avoidance of the experiential realm. As a result of increasing specialization, of course, a discipline often splits into subdomains among which there is decreasing direct communication. The subdomains may then become recognized as distinct disciplines, each more restricted in scope than the parent discipline. It is conceivable that the increasing specialization of interests that we see in psychology will ultimately lead to this end.

The third class of changes I have outlined above encompasses a great variety of possibilities, some of them quite subtle in manifestation. The first subcategory listed, replacement, can be regarded as a combination of expansion and restriction. Old areas, methods, and issues are abandoned at the same time that new ones are adopted. It is obvious that this kind of change occurs with respect to many of the ingredients of any science. The issues and concerns of 1950 or 1970 are not the same as those of 1900. If we represent the basic

modes of variation in orientation within a discipline by a system of
dimensions, replacement could be manifested in either of two ways
in the dimensional system. If we arrive at the dimensions by cross-
sectional analysis—by doing separate analyses at different moments
in time—we may find that the system of dimensions itself changes.
Some dimensions vanish and others appear to take their place.
Another possibility is something I have called *factor metamorphosis*.
In this case, we have the same dimensions or factors, but there is
change within these. In the factors studied in the personality realm,
we see this kind of change with respect to forms of expression. A
factor of dominance or assertiveness that is manifested in bodily
clashes among small children may be expressed in the adolescent or
adult in more subtle forms of social control. In the history of
psychology, we can see the same kind of change within many dimensions. Perhaps *endogenism vs. exogenism* would be a good example.
At all points in history, we find some people who look for external or
environmental sources of human action and experience, while others
look for inner sources—whether in terms of instincts, genes, individual constitution, or physiological process. The terms, the methods,
and the specific subject matter studied have all changed, but the
polarity remains. In some form, the related nature-nurture issue
remains, but it is not likely to be stated now in the same form as it
would have been 50 or 100 years ago.

The other subcategories I noted above involve various changes
in the organization or alignment of issues. What I have called convergence or integration would entail an increase in the relatedness
or interpenetration of certain issues. Issues that might have been
seen as unrelated are brought increasingly into a common context,
so that an emphasis on a particular subject matter comes to be seen
as tied to a particular kind of method and linked in turn to certain
modes of conceptualization. Viewed in terms of statistical consequences, this means that issues that have been uncorrelated become
increasingly correlated. As a result, it becomes possible to describe
individuals not simply in terms of their standing on a host of specific
issues, but in terms of a dimension of variation that is common to
the issues. If we think in terms of the consequences for a multivariate analysis of the domain, the result may be either factor
emergence or factor convergence. In the former case, specific variables become increasingly correlated, and factor analysis may yield
a factor loading the whole set of variables where there was no factor
that could be isolated at an earlier time. In the case of factor convergence, the integration takes place on a more general level. Factors that were present earlier become increasingly correlated and

form a higher-level factor. If they converge sufficiently, the original factors vanish, and the broader higher-order factor displaces them at the first-order level.

Divergence or disintegration would imply just the opposite course. Issues become more independent of one another. A method ceases to be tied to a particular theoretical outlook, and its application is no longer confined to a particular subject matter. A particular subject matter interest ceases to be tied to a particular theoretical viewpoint, and the subject matter itself is conceptualized in a greater variety of ways. The result in this case is a decrease in the correlations within a set of variables. A broad factor may split into factors of more specific content. The more specific factors become decreasingly correlated with one another. As very specific issues cease to be correlated with one another, a factor may dissolve altogether. I have previously spoken of these processes in terms of *factor divergence* and *factor disintegration*.

The one other possibility I have listed is reorganization. By this I mean any realignment of issues that does not necessarily result in a change in the number of dimensions of the system. We could think of this as a combination of convergence and divergence. Issue A becomes more independent of issue B but at the same time more closely tied to issue C. This can happen as old issues die in old contexts and are resurrected in new ones. Or it can happen as methodological issues or arguments about modes of conceptualization are transported from one subject matter area to another. In this case, the total pattern of intercorrelations is altered. Some correlations increase, while others decrease. In an extreme case, we might find the sort of change in the character of isolable dimensions that I described above with respect to replacement. On a more modest scale, we may find essentially the same factors or dimensions when we perform an analysis, but we find that some of the variables move from one factor to another. A variable that was most highly loaded by factor A is now loaded only by factor B, while one of the variables that was loaded by B now fits into a cluster of variables loaded by C, etc. I have previously called this kind of change *factor component interchange*.

I have described all these possible kinds of change not because we need them to conceptualize the evidence now available on trends in psychology, but because we may need them if we are going to deal with historical trends in a comprehensive way. Perhaps most of the casual descriptions of changes in psychology have emphasized shifts in central tendency and expansion, but that is simply because it is relatively easy to spot gross changes of these kinds. It is my hope that by developing instruments like the Theoretical Orientation Survey we can study shifts in central tendency still more systematically, comparing data collected from a succession of samples over time. Some of the other kinds of possible change, however, may call for methods of data collection and analysis that no one has attempted. At the very least, an adequate study of changes in the composition of the total system of variables pertaining to theoretical orientation would call for a series of factor analyses of data collected for successive periods in the past history of psychology, as well as for the periods yet to come.

DESCRIPTIONS AND PRESCRIPTIONS

Before considering some of the findings yielded by my own research, I should like to consider some of the ways in which other people have characterized historical trends in psychology. I have not attempted a comprehensive survey of historical analyses, but I think that the few analyses I shall note here will serve to illustrate both the common threads and the variations to be found in such analyses. There have been many descriptions of change in psychology based on content analyses of periodical literature. One of the most thorough analyses of this type was published by Bruner and Allport in 1940.[2] Bruner and Allport examined the content of articles in 14 leading psychological journals for every tenth year from 1888 to 1938. For each article published, they considered the author's problem, his presuppositions, his procedure, his explanatory concepts, and his outlook on psychological science. They classified the articles in terms of 32 categories.

For each of the 32 categories, Bruner and Allport report a comparison of the six years that they analyzed. (Actually, they report only five sets of results, since the data were combined for 1888 and 1898.) The most conspicuous trends apparent in their data include the following:

1. An increase in the use of animal subjects
2. An increase in the study of higher mental processes through nonlinguistic responses
3. A decrease in the study of higher mental processes through linguistic responses
4. An increase in the use of statistics
5. A decrease in the facultative treatment of mental and neural functions
6. A decrease in treatment of the body-mind problem (ac-

companied by a tendency to deny the existence of the
problem while making implicit assumptions about it)
7. An increase in discussions of statistical methodology
8. An increase in mention of operationism
9. An increase in formal conceptual analysis or in
"methodological positivism"

Most of these could be characterized as shifts in central tendency, though Bruner and Allport feel that their data also provide
evidence of two opposed trends in 1938. One of these emphasizes
"psychology for science's sake" and is expressed in animal and
physiological research, rigorous methodology, a pursuit of basic science, and a shunning of concern with social significance. The other
emphasizes "psychology for society's sake" and is expressed in an
increased concern with human values and social research and a concern for concepts with relevance for the problems of everyday life. In
some respects, these opposing trends correspond to a diversification
of interests among psychologists. For essentially the same historical
period, Fernberger found evidence of an increase in interest in both
physiological psychology and social psychology.[3] This kind of change
could best be regarded as a case of expansion. On the other hand,
some of the manifestations of this opposition observed by Bruner and
Allport probably point to a rising salience of issues on which viewpoints conflict.

Many of the trends noted by Bruner and Allport have undoubtedly continued in the same direction into the 1970s, while others
have not. Psychologists have used an increasingly greater variety of
animal subjects, but I suspect that currently the proportion of total
experimental studies utilizing animal subjects is declining. Perhaps
the peaks in that proportion was reached in the 1940s or 1950s. Noting the shift from linguistic responses to nonlinguistic responses in
the study of higher mental processes, Allport notes that "the distinctively human function of language has a decreasing appeal for
psychologists, even when the language expression is in the form of
standardized tests."[4] Perhaps this was true up until 1938 or 1940.
The field of psycholinguistics has undergone most of its development
since then. In summarizing all the findings of the study, Allport
says that psychology has become increasingly empirical, mechanistic, quantitative, nomothetic, analytic, and operational. If these
trends are not all still in progress, we could still probably apply this
description to the changes that have occurred through most of the
years from 1940 to the present.

In principle, the content analysis of published literature is an eminently sound way of undertaking an historical analysis of a science, but the choice of content categories is only one of the obvious methodological problems entailed. A more difficult problem is that of securing an appropriate sample of literature. Ideally, we would want a fully comprehensive sample—all the literature published in the field. But how do we define the boundaries of the field? Which books and journals are properly within the domain of the science of psychology, and which ones are not? Bruner and Allport were able to choose 14 journals that they felt represented scientific psychology and used these for the entire period covered by their study. If this was a satisfactory route for the period from 1888 to 1938, it would probably be less satisfactory for the period since then. Journals have proliferated at an increasing rate, and every time a new journal has appeared in a growing area of specialization, its appearance has had an impact on the content of journals already in existence. An article that might once have been most appropriate for the *Psychological Review,* the *Psychological Bulletin,* or the *American Psychologist* may now be considered more suitable for the *Journal of the History of the Behavioral Sciences.* Quite independently of the emergence of new journals, of course, shifting editorial policies may differentially affect the acceptability of articles of various types and contents. In a sense, a science *is* its published literature, but it may be very difficult to sample this literature in a way that will ideally serve the purposes of historical research.

Many historical analysts have followed the much different route of attempting to discern the trends represented by the more global shifts apparent in major movements in psychology and in the thinking of leading theorists. In the first chapter, I noted the work of one of the most discerning of these analysts, Egon Brunswik.[5] Brunswik distinguishes two basic issues underlying theory, and with respect to each of these he feels there has been a monotonic progression in the development of psychology. He sees a more or less continuous progression from subjectivism to objectivism, and at the same time he sees a development from a static and molecular approach to a dynamic and molar type of approach.

Madsen presents a comparable type of analysis and apparently agrees in part with Brunswik.[6] He analyzes the structure of 20 theories of motivation, compares them in terms of six basic modes of classification, and makes the following observations with respect to observed and probable trends:

1. There has been a trend toward more exact and systematic theory construction.

2. There was an era of constructive theory initiated by Tolman, followed by an era of reductive theory initiated by Hebb. Further movement toward reductive theory is likely.

3. The great contrast between mentalistic and behavioristic theories evident in the period from 1910 to 1930 has been superseded by a higher synthesis in the form of neutral-formal theories.

4. There has been a movement toward more molar theories, and future developments will probably continue in the same direction.

5. Theories of a field-theoretical type of probably supersede theories of a mechanistic type and theories of a dynamic type.

6. In place of theories of a statistical type or deterministic type, we will probably see more theories of an intermediate (probability-deterministic) form.

The fourth observation agrees with Brunswik's views. If we can equate the mentalistic-behavioristic dichotomy with subjectivism-objectivism, the third point is in conflict with Brunswik's position. Madsen sees a synthesis where Brunswik does not. Perhaps most of the theoretical systems that Madsen calls neutral-formal would be classified by Brunswik as objectivistic, but we lack the details we would need for a detailed comparison of the categories employed by Brunswik and Madsen. The theoretical territory embraced by such terms as subjectivistic and objectivistic is so vast that we can undoubtedly find within it issues on which syntheses have been achieved as well as issues on which there has simply been a linear trend.

The synthesis suggested by Madsen involves a kind of change that cannot be described as a shift in central tendency. It would be a situation in which an issue ceases to be a focus of controversy because the previously opposed positions both cease to be viable. If the issue has been so central as to form the basis for a major dimension of theory, the dimension may lose variance and disappear, perhaps to be superseded by new dimensions—an instance of what I have called replacement. The notion of synthesis was also a part of Brunswik's thinking, for as a one-time student of Brunswik, I recall that he once suggested in a lecture that perhaps every major turning point in the history of science could be characterized as the resolution of a dichotomy. This is certainly not a new idea, since it has long been around in the form of a triadic dialectic formula that has usually been attributed to Hegel. According to this formula, the existence of one condition or idea, the thesis, evokes a contrary idea, the antithesis, and the interaction of the two leads ultimately to a synthesis. From the synthesis a new opposition, different from the earlier one, may arise. We can undoubtedly describe some, but certainly not all, of the historical sequences in science in terms of this formula.

Quite apart from the triadic formula, of course, it is possible to view the development or history of a discipline in terms of a sequence of dominant ideas or motifs. This notion has aroused wide discussion in the last few years in the form presented by Thomas Kuhn.[7] Kuhn's basic thesis is that the development of a science cannot be adequately described in terms of a process of accumulation or accretion. It is better understood in terms of a succession of paradigms. Kuhn fails to define *paradigm* in any precise way, and his examples suggest meanings that range from fairly circumscribed research hypotheses to grand world views that pervade all aspects of thought in a given discipline. However one may choose to delineate this concept further, Kuhn evidently intends to refer to a fairly comprehensive schema or way of viewing things that for a period of time dominates the thinking of a science. In periods of "normal science" the paradigm is generally accepted and researchers proceed in a more or less orderly way to acquire facts that are illuminated by it and to elaborate on the paradigm itself. There are also occasional periods of "extraordinary science" when confidence in the paradigm breaks down—as a result of a persistent failure to solve noteworthy puzzles or to account for anomalous facts—and a shift to a new paradigm ensues. Kuhn contends that the paradigm determines to a great extent how we see the world. It determines to a great extent what we are able to recognize as "facts," and a shift from one paradigm to another is analogous to a shift in the perception of an ambiguous figure (a "Gestalt switch").

The application of Kuhn's idea to psychology has become a matter of lively debate. In the natural sciences it is possible to identify some major paradigms and paradigm shifts of truly comprehensive scope, e.g., the advent of atomic theory and the shift from a Ptolemaic to a Copernican view of the universe. In psychology, there appear to be no motifs of comparable scale, and the tendency of most writers has been to conclude that psychology is still in a very early stage of development. Kuhn speaks of preparadigmatic stages, when there is much competition among distinctly different views of nature. When the thinking in an immature but developing field reaches a certain level of maturity, a unifying paradigm may arise and provide the foundation for a coherent tradition of research. If psychology lacks the sort of grand view that constitutes a true paradigm, perhaps it is still in its infancy. Perhaps it will undergo more rapid progress when it achieves a paradigm.

Is this a valid assessment of the *corpus psychologicum?* Perhaps there has not been anything quite comparable to the Copernican revolution in psychology, though the theories of Darwin and Freud have certainly been regarded by many people as providing the impetus for comparable revolutions. Perhaps psychology is not a very unified science, but it is nonetheless possible to find a few ideas and themes that have dominated important theoretical and research traditions within it. Evolutionary doctrine, as formulated by Darwin and modified by his successors, has been such a theme. It not only colors our thinking about the biological underpinnings of human behavior and experience, but also strongly affects our views of the adjustment process and learning. The Skinnerian view of learning is essentially an application of the notion of natural selection to the realm of behavioral ontogeny. In the developmental realm, evolutionary doctrine has appeared most often in the notion that increasing complexity results from the interaction of simultaneous processes of differentiation and integration. As I have noted elsewhere, this formula can be and has been applied to creative processes of many different kinds.[8] For its application to human development and social change, we are largely indebted to Herbert Spencer, who was perhaps the most gifted theoretical mind among Darwin's associates.

It is possible to identify still other ideas and themes of broad scope that have dominated important traditions in psychology. Obvious examples would include *unconscious motivation, conditioned reflex,* and *Gestalt.* If psychologists at large ever awaken fully to the significance of Jungian theory, perhaps we can add *archetype* to the list. Still, it can be argued that none of these ideas has quite the scope required for qualification as a true paradigm, though it is not at all clear how we are to determine that. Given this premise, at any rate, there are those who feel that we should seek a unifying paradigm. Albert Gilgen believes that it is both possible and desirable to achieve a unified science and that systems theory can provide the basis for it.[9] The integrating paradigm would be a hierarchical feedback model of organisms-in-their-environments. He believes that a number of trends currently evident in psychology point to this kind of model as the sort of idea to which psychologists are likely to turn in the years to come and in which they can find a common ground for communication and scientific progress.

A sharply contrasting view is expressed by Sigmund Koch, who contends that psychology cannot possibly be a coherent discipline.[10] He believes that the nature of the subject matter, in contrast to that of many of the natural sciences, is such that a diversity of languages is inevitable in psychology. He argues that the history of psychology indicates an overall tendency toward theoretical and substantive fractionation and specialization, not integration. He predicts further isolation of specialized communities within psychology. According to Koch, a misreading of Kuhn has generated a false optimism among psychologists and spurred them to seek some magical formula that will transform psychology into a mature, progressive science. Koch feels that the hope that systems theory can provide the remedy for our schisms is illusory. He says the notion of a comprehensive *general* systems theory is at best a fragile metaphor. Rather than providing a means of achieving theoretical syntheses and facilitating communication among psychologists, the advocacy of such an idea is tantamount to a global prescription that we search for isomorphisms (which is what all scientists inevitably do anyway).

We have now seen a variety of readings of the history of psychology and of current trends. It is interesting that most of these readings tend to be accompanied by prescriptions for actions that can shape the future. Brunswik saw psychology becoming more objectivistic and molar and regarded the trend as desirable. The sort of molar objectivism represented by the work of Tolman was an ideal to be sought. Allport saw psychology becoming more empirical, mechanistic, quantitative, nomothetic, analytic, and operational and feared that the end result might prove too lopsided. He saw creative potential in diversity and recommended that we also allow psychology to be rational, telelogical, qualitative, idiographic, synoptic, and nonoperational. Allport advocated tolerance or cultivation of a perspective that has come to be known as humanistic. An advocacy of humanistic psychology is seen in a host of more recent publications, e.g., in the work of Maslow.

Some humanistic psychologists see their view as embracing— rather than opposing—positions that are better established in the academic world. They see a need for theory that will incoporate the insights of both humanists and behaviorists. Presumably, too, the sort of unifying edifice envisioned by people like Gilgen would utilize building blocks cut by various factions that now appear to be in conflict. On the other hand, many behaviorists would probably see such a future as a dilution of their science, and objections come from other quarters as well. Hebb thinks it is a mistake to seek a humanistic psychology, for humanism and science represent two different (but equally legitimate and fruitful) ways of knowing human beings, and they really cannot be mixed.[11] We should stick to the path of objective science.

Koch's complaints rest on a much different foundation. He sees a uniform mixture as impossible, but like Allport, he sees value in diversity. He thinks we should accept our diversity, and encourage people to use whatever methods and concepts best suit their special areas within psychology. As a result, in some subdomains psychology may resemble the arts, while in others it may look like physics or biology. Hebb fears that in trying to be simultaneously scientific and humanistic we shall fall between two stools, but Koch believes that psychology is the polymorphous discipline that can bridge the gap between the two.

I find I am largely in agreement with Koch on this matter. His reading of the heterogeneous character of psychology seems to me to be correct, and I am not certain there is much to be gained by wishing it were otherwise. The route advocated by Hebb and by staunch behaviorists seems to me a conservative clinging to disciplinary distinctions that serve to inhibit fruitful cross-fertilizations. I think we will see repeated efforts toward the achievement of higher syntheses of diverse insights and viewpoints. I think that some humanistic psychologists, following in Maslow's footsteps, will work toward this end. There will also be efforts to effect syntheses with systems concepts, and perhaps this will prove more fruitful than Koch foresees. While systems theory may not contain the grand paradigm, it may still serve a heuristic role by providing a way of looking for the paradigm. Perhaps the pick that was meant to strike a vein of gold will at least unearth a few chunks of silver.

RESEARCH EVIDENCE ON HISTORICAL TRENDS

In Chapter 2, we considered a factor analysis of 34 theoretical variables applied to 54 major theorists. The research data on which that analysis was based also provided a basis for examining historical trends. As I noted, the list of 54 theorists had been drawn from a much longer list on the basis of judges' ratings. The judges had been asked both to rate all names in terms of overall importance of contributions to psychological theory and in terms of importance of contributions within each decade from the 1880s to the 1950s. The list of 54 consisted of those who were either among the top 50 in overall ratings or among the top 10 for any decade.

The analysis yielded six factors, and in the course of it, I derived factor scores for all 54 theorists by multiple regression. To examine historical trends, I took the scores for the top 10 theorists of each decade and averaged them for each of the six factors. The results are shown in Table 3. In the rating study, the six factors were construed as follows:

1. Subjectivism vs. objectivism
2. Holism vs. elementarism
3. Apersonal vs. personal orientation
4. Quantitative vs. qualitative orientation
5. Dynamic vs. static orientation
6. Endogenism vs. exogenism

The clearest trend of all is that for factor 1, which shows a progressive movement from subjectivism to objectivism. This is consistent with the data of Bruner and Allport, and it supports Brunswik's analysis. In the related factor of *quantitative vs. qualitative orientation,* however, we see a somewhat different temporal pattern. It is basically U-shaped, with a low point in the 1930s, but from there the trend is sharply upward, leading to the highest mean in the 1950s. If we think of factor 4 as representing objectivism with respect to methodology, it provides only partial support for Brunswik's analysis.

With respect to *holism vs. elementarism,* which logically corresponds to molar vs. molecular orientation, the evidence is less supportive, for here the overall trend is clearly an inverted-U trend. The holistic peak is reached in the 1920s. The remaining three factors show trends that are somewhat more irregular. For factor 3, *apersonal vs. personal orientation,* an initial dip is followed by an upward trend. For the last four periods, we see a plateau at an elevation well above any of the first four periods; so the overall trend is from personal to apersonal. In factor 5 there is an almost monotonic progression from the static to the dynamic. The one reversal occurs from the 1910s to the 1920s. In factor 6, initial fluctuation leads to an endogenist peak in the period from 1910 to 1919, and from that point onward, we see a monotonic progression toward exogenism.

We can secure a few additional insights into the nature of these changes by looking at the trends for the 34 specific variables from which the factors were derived. These variables were originally rated on a five-point scale, in which the extremes of $+2$ and -2 represent marked positive emphasis and marked rejection respectively and 0 represents the neutral point. For purposes of data processing, a constant of 2.00 was added, and each rating was expressed in terms of scale from 0 to 4. If we average the ratings on each variable for the top 10 theorists for each decade, we obtain the results shown in Table 4.

It is fairly easy to sort the 34 variables into a number of distinct groups in terms of profile or pattern of change. It is convenient to think of these groups in terms of four basic pattern types. I shall speak of type A when the change approximates a monotonic upward progression and type B when the change approximates a monotonic progression in a downward direction. Types C and D would be curvilinear progressions that end at about the same level where they begin. Type C would be an inverted U pattern, while type D would be a straight U pattern.

As we would expect, the essentially monotonic progressions are most characteristic of those variables that are loaded by factors 1 and 5. The variables that come close to the type A pattern of upward progression include:

1. Learning
3. Motivation
5. Observable behavior
10. Social determinants of behavior
12. Influence of past experience on behavior
13. Immediate external determinants of behavior
23. Determinism
26. Operational definition of concepts
29. Nomothetic approach

There are four variables that come close to the type B pattern:

4. Conscious processes, conscious experience
17. Introspective reports
20. "Armchair" speculation
22. Voluntarism

Obviously the increases shown for the first group and the decline shown for the second can be largely rationalized in terms of a movement from subjectivism to objectivism.

There are four variables that fit the type C pattern rather well, reaching peaks somewhere in the middle periods:

9. Biological determinants
15. Uniqueness of individual personality
16. Persisting traits of individuals

28. Holism

There are two variables that show the reverse pattern—
that of type D.

30. Normative generalization
31. Quantitative formulation of principles and relationships

The remaining variables all show somewhat greater departure
from any single type pattern, though most of them may be said to
involve type combinations. To consider first those variables that
show an overall pattern that is more upward than downward, we
can see two variables that fit what we might call an AC type pattern. The overall trend is upward, but the pattern shows a terminal
decline:

14. Total organization of behavior
33. Conceptualization in terms of hypothetical entities

There is also a pattern that we might call AD. Despite an initial
decline, the overall trend is upward:

18. Rigidly controlled experimentation
19. Statistical analysis
25. Mechanism
32. Quantitative description of individuals and behavior

Variables 13, 26, and 29, which I placed in the type A group are
borderline cases. We might consider them either A or AD.
    There are three variables that fit a type BC group. Here the
overall trend, despite an initial rise, is downward:

11. Heredity, constitution
21. Naturalistic observation
24. Finalism

Two other variables manifest a curious variation on this pattern,
both having elevations for the second and fourth decades with a dip
between these:

6. Unconscious processes
8. Self-concept, self-perception

There are two other variables that show a BD pattern—a terminal rise in a pattern that is otherwise downward:

2. Sensation and perception
27. Elementarism

There are two other variables, and both of these come closer than the rest to displaying a complete wave form. This form is clearest for variable 34 (use of analogies based on physical systems), where the pattern drops to a low point in the 1890s, rises to a peak in the 1920s, and finally ends slightly below the initial level. Variable 7 (emotion) shows a more shallow wave form of the reverse pattern.

There is probably not much point in pondering further about the precise form of any of these patterns, for they rest on a limited sample of information. They can best be taken to represent genuine trends for the field of psychology as a whole where we see a progression of sizable increases or decreases, particularly where the trend continues monotonically for the entire period studied—as in factor 1 and variable 17. Even then, it would be folly to extrapolate from the observed pattern and assume that the same sort of trend is likely to continue indefinitely. For most of the factors and variables at hand, cyclic variation might be a more reasonable expectation. Each of the variables represents a topic, a procedure, or a perspective that has something to offer us in our efforts to make sense of our observations of the human scene, and we might well expect a period in which a particular variable is either neglected or markedly emphasized to be followed by a swing in a contrary direction. To the extent that thesis and antithesis tend to be concurrent rather than successive, of course, the compensatory accent will not be apparent in a series of mean values. We would need to look for simultaneous opposing trends, which might be better reflected in measures of variance than in measures of central tendency. We would probably need to study a larger sample of theorists to capture definite trends in variance or salience with much fidelity.

We can gain a few further insights into the trends we have just seen by considering the theorists who are actually represented by these data. At the same time, the reader may find it useful to see what factor scores were obtained for each theorist. These values are expressed in Table 5 in the form of T scores. The theorists are shown in descending order with respect to the mean ratings assigned them for the overall importance of their contributions to psychological theory.

Perhaps the astute reader could predict many of the trends we have considered above by simply noting which theorists obtained the top 10 mean ratings for each decade. I shall report these in descending order of mean rating for the decade. In other words, in each of the following lists, the name given first is that of the theorist whose contributions during that decade were rated most highly:

1880–1889: Wundt, James, Helmholtz, Ebbinghaus, Fechner, Galton, Charcot, Brentano, Müller, Mach.

1890–1899: James, Wundt, Dewey, Titchener, Freud, Janet, Ebbinghaus, Galton, Hall, Külpe.

1900–1909: Freud, Titchener, Thorndike, Binet, Pavlov, McDougall, Sherrington, Dewey, Angell, Wundt.

1910–1919: Watson, Wertheimer, Freud, Thorndike, Pavlov, McDougall, Köhler, Spearman, Jung, Adler.

1920–1929: Freud, Watson, Köhler, Pavlov, Thorndike, Wertheimer, Lewin, Lashley, Koffka, Adler.

1930–1939: Hull, Tolman, Lewin, Freud, Köhler, Lashley, Allport, Thorndike, Skinner, Guthrie.

1940–1949: Hull, Tolman, Skinner, Lewin, Rogers, Hebb, Köhler, Miller, Spence, Thurstone.

1950–1959: Skinner, Hebb, Harlow, Miller, Spence, Mowrer, Brunswik, Rogers, Tolman, Estes.

In the light of these lists and the information provided in Table 5, we can see that the trend toward objectivism seen in factor 1 is essentially a trend in experimental psychology. Experimental psychologists dominate in the later decade lists, and they tend to score low on factor 1. In general, clinical and personality theorists tend to score high, as do the early experimentalists. The highest scores, of course, are those for McDougall and Jung.

For factor 2, we found an inverted-U trend with a peak for the decade 1920–1929. In the middle periods, we see high scores in this factor associated with McDougall, Lewin, Wertheimer, Köhler, and Koffka. More than anything else, the holistic peak represents the influence of Gestalt psychology during those periods.

In the case of factor 3, we find scores toward the personal end of the continuum generally for clinical-personality theorists, as well as a few nonclinicians such as Hall and Binet. An upward trend in scores is partly a function of the fact that academic-experimental theorists are more predominant in the later decade lists.

Factor 4 shows a U trend, and the trough in the middle periods may be ascribed in part to the same influences that govern the peak for factor 2. Low scores in these periods are found for Freud, Adler, Jung, McDougall, and the Gestalt psychologists.

The upward trend in factor 5 represents in large part a movement away from the concerns of the early experimentalists to an increasing concern with processes of various kinds. The scores of the early decades seem rather widely dispersed compared with recent decades. Some high scores appear early. In terms of the extreme scores, this is actually a McDougall vs. Titchener factor.

In factor 6, we see initial fluctuation followed by a monotonic progression toward exogenism from the 1920s through the 1950s. The exogenist trend seems to be associated with the prominence in the later decade lists of theorists focally concerned with the learning process. It is my impression that learning theory per se is receiving decreasing emphasis in psychology now, and I suspect that if we brought this study up to date we would find a reversal of the exogenist trend—notwithstanding the current influence of both Skinner and the social learning theorists. It is always hazardous to try to read ongoing trends, however, because there are so many things happening at once. When we operate retrospectively, we have the simpler task of identifying those events that have had lasting effects.

There have been a number of developments since 1959 that might affect any current or future follow-up of this research. The humanistic movement in psychology has received increased attention. Some humanistic theorists such as Gordon Allport, Carl Rogers, and Erich Fromm had already enjoyed considerable popularity, but in the 1960s a variety of others either emerged into view or achieved increasing recognition—Erik Erikson, Abraham Maslow, Rollo May, and Fritz Perls. Carl Jung, who remains the greatest theorist of this tradition, has begun to receive a bit more attention than he used to receive. At the same time, a sharply contrasting movement of social engineering has blossomed forth, the most conspicuous figures in this development being B. F. Skinner and social learning theorists such as Albert Bandura. Both of these movements have attracted considerable attention outside the academic world and outside professional psychology. The most ardent followers of the leading contemporary humanists are likely to be found outside the ranks of the American Psychological Association.

There are many other developments of the 1960s and 1970s that may change the shape of psychology. There have been many developments in cognitive psychology and psycholinguistics. In the fields of cognitive and developmental psychology, Jean Piaget, certainly a better theorist than any contemporary American psychologist, has finally received a bit of belated recognition in this country.

We can get a rough idea of shifts in the influence of various theorists by comparing the lists of theorists shown in Table 5 with one based on a more recent compilation. The list in Table 5 is based on data gathered in 1960 and 1961. In 1972, I distributed the Theoretical Orientation Survey to about 3000 members of the American Psychological Association. One of the items appended to the orientation questions was the question: "What prominent theorist comes closest to representing the views that you espouse in psychological theory? (The theorist may or may not be contemporary and may or may not be primarily identified as a psychologist. Do not write your own name.)"

This item elicited a highly varied set of responses. Many respondents failed to follow the directions. Of 866 psychologists who returned the form over 100 declined to respond at all to this item. A great number of those who did respond gave multiple answers. The names that were written in response to the item numbered altogether in the hundreds. There were very few that appeared with conspicuous frequency. The following names appeared five or more times as single entries. In parentheses after each name, I have indicated first the number of times it appeared singly and then the number of times it appeared in combination with one or more other names:

B. F. Skinner (63, 24)
S. Freud (56, 14)
C. R. Rogers (51, 32)
J. Piaget (39, 14)
K. Lewin (27, 10)
A. H. Maslow (24, 16)
E. H. Erikson (24, 11)
G. W. Allport (19, 6)
H. S. Sullivan (18, 8)
F. Perls (14, 11)
A. Adler (13, 7)
C. G. Jung (10, 7)
D. O. Hebb (9, 6)
C. L. Hull (9, 4)
G. A. Kelly (9, 4)
W. Glasser (8, 4)
W. James (8, 2)
A. Lazarus (8, 1)

K. W. Spence (8, 1)
E. C. Tolman (8, 1)
N. E. Miller (7, 7)
A. Bandura (7, 4)
G. Murphy (6, 2)
J. Rotter (5, 3)
K. Horney (5, 1)

In comparing this list with the earlier one, we must remember that the difference between them is not just a function of the time at which data were collected. The task assigned to respondents was much different. In the later study, they were asked to name theorists with views close to their own. In the earlier study, they rated theorists in terms of importance of contributions, and presumably they often assigned high ratings to theorists with whom they sharply disagreed. The later data sampling is much more dependent on the climate of opinion and interests at the time of the study.

Another basic difference lies in the nature of the respondent sample. In the earlier study, the respondents were nearly all academic psychologists were strong interests in history and systems. In the later study, they were essentially a cross section of APA membership. They thus included far more people with applied interests, particularly in the clinical area.

Bearing these considerations in mind, we can still discern some current trends by examining the later list and comparing it with the earlier one. Skinner and Piaget are both much higher on this list than they would have been if we had posed the same question 10 years earlier, and Hull is considerably lower. In the theoretical-importance ratings, Freud and Hull came out in first and second place respectively. I think Freud would still be at the top if I repeated that study, for he has certainly established himself as the most influential theorist in the history of psychology. Hull's position, however, would undoubtedly shift, for his influence has waned considerably since 1960. Skinner has obviously displaced Hull as the leading hero of objectivistic psychologists.

Skinner emerges in the later study as the single most popular theorist at the present time, and there is certainly no other behaviorist of comparable prominence. At the same time, there is no single humanistic psychologist who commands quite the attention that Skinner does, though Rogers comes closest. We should note, however, that there are a number of less conspicous heroes in the humanistic camp, and those who ally themselves with Skinner are definitely outnumbered by those who identify more closely with one of the humanistic theorists. Behaviorism may be a dominant influence in academic psychology, but psychologists at large lean much more strongly in a humanistic direction. It is obvious, nonetheless, that objectivistic and subjectivistic forms of psychology are both very much alive, and we can probably expect these contrasting trends to continue well into the future.

The list also provides ample testimony to the immense durability of Sigmund Freud, though I suspect that if this study has been done a few years earlier he would have shown a more commanding lead over everyone else. Just as interest has shifted from Hull to Skinner within some camps, it has shifted from Freud to more humanistic theorists within other camps. While these two shifts in combination represent a divergence of views in some respects, they also suggest a pervasive decline in emphasis on formal theory. Both Skinner and the existentialists (a salient influence in the humanistic movement) have called for some sort of "empiricism." Admittedly, radical behaviorism and gnosticism do not look very much alike, but they both represent alternatives to a heavy reliance on rational analysis and abstract conceptualization. They both favor greater reliance on immediate evidence, while differing in the way they conceive of such evidence.

One further ingredient of the current climate is suggested by the nature of some of the combinations provided by respondents who wrote in more than one name. Most of these represented theoretically coherent mixtures, such as Bruner and Piaget or Perls, Laing, and May. There were a number of combinations that seemed rather discordant, however, the most common being Rogers and Skinner. In some cases, this combination may have reflected the naiveté of the respondent, but perhaps more often it was given by a respondent who felt that basic theoretical issues were much less important than ideas that could be applied to the world of practical human affairs. This sort of pragmatic outlook does not appear to be represented among the patterns of orientation thus far isolated by statistical analysis.

5. Demographic and Professional Variables

THE SEARCH FOR CORRELATES OF THEORETICAL ORIENTATION

In 1972, in an effort to study correlates of theoretical orientation and to gain insights into both its effects and its determinants, I mailed copies of the Theoretical Orientation Survey to almost 3000 members of the American Psychological Association. My initial procedure in selecting correspondents was simply to take names consecutively from the APA Directory, starting at the point where I had stopped in the preceding stage of my research. It was obvious, however, that if I selected all names in order as I proceeded through the pages of the directory, I would end up with a sample in which the men would outnumber the women by a ratio of well over 3 to 1. Recognizing that sex differences might be appreciable in some of the variables and relationships that I intended to study, I altered my procedure before drawing my entire sample and beyond a certain point took from the directory only names that I presumed to be feminine.

There appeared to be no sex difference in return rates. Of the 866 people who returned the TOS answer form, 510 were men and 356 were women. Compared to the total membership of the APA, this sample contains a relatively large proportion of women. Apart from the sex ratio and apart from the biases introduced by the correspondent's decision either to participate or not to do so, the total sample should be representative of the APA population.

The TOS form itself contained spaces to record sex, age, and responses to several items pertaining to professional activities and interests, but it seemed unwise to seek too much information at once. I asked respondents, in filling out the form, to indicate whether they were willing to fill out additional forms. Most of the respondents indicated that they were willing. In assembling a battery of instruments that could be related to TOS variables, I hoped to gain a more comprehensive picture of the people who manifested each basic pattern of theoretical orientation. I focused on biographical, attitudinal, and personality variables and selected a combination of instruments that promised a suitable composite picture. The total battery contained 10 instruments, and it would have been rather unreasonable to expect any subject to complete all of these. Therefore, it was divided into four subsets, and every respondent who volunteered to provide more information was sent only one of these.

One of the subsets included a biographical questionnaire,[1] the Roe-Siegelman Parent-Child-Relations Questionnaire,[2] and the Survey of Interpersonal Values.[3] A second subset included the Sixteen Personality Factor Questionnaire[4] and the Personal Opinion Survey.[5] A third subset included the Myers-Briggs Type Indicator[6] and the Experience Inventory.[7] The fourth subset included the Allport-Vernon-Lindzey Study of Values,[8] the General Beliefs questionnaire,[9] and the Psycho-Epistemological Profile.[10] Most of the subjects who received additional questionnaires completed them and returned them, though the demands of the task may have exceeded their initial expectations. Perhaps it should be noted that the indication of willingness to complete the additional forms correlated essentially zero with all the factors of theoretical orientation. This suggests that the relatively small samples used in the later stages of this research, despite the effects of successive attrition, are still reasonably representative of the APA population.

SEX, AGE, AND PROFESSIONAL ACTIVITY

The TOS forms that were completed and returned provided the normative data presented in the tables in the Appendix. A comparison of those tables will show that appreciable sex differences are evident for most of the factors. On the average, men score higher on all factors except 5 *(biological determinism)* and II *(endogenism)*. The latter difference, favoring higher scores for women on endogenism, barely fails to reach the 5% level of significance. Women do score significantly higher than men on *biological determinism*.

The most marked differences are found for *objectivism* and its components, particularly *impersonal causality*. All these differences favor more objectivistic scores for men. Thus, in comparison with women, men score high on *impersonal causality, behavioral content emphasis, elementarism, physicalism,* and *quantitative orientation*. With respect to theoretical orientation women tend to be more oriented to the personal and subjective realm. There is also a small difference on factor 1, which is more weakly loaded by *objectivism*.

On that factor, men tend more strongly than women toward factual orientation. Perhaps we should note that with samples of this size, a rather small difference can be statistically significant. Indeed, all the sex differences we observe here are small relative to the variation within each sex.

All the factors except 6 *(environmental determinism)* and 8 *(quantitative orientation)* show small significant correlations with age. *Objectivism* correlates $-.150$ with age, and all its components manifest correlations consistent with this. Thus, older subjects tend to be more subjectivistic, more theoretically oriented, more will oriented, more experiential-content oriented, more holistic, and less physicalistic. There are basically two ways in which we might interpret the association between age and the objectivism-subjectivism polarity. It may represent a genuine generational trend. This would mean that psychologists as a scientific population are becoming progressively more objectivistic (or that they have done so up till now). This may be true, for it is consistent with the temporal trend that emerged in the research on major theorists.

The other possibility is that we are seeing a developmental effect—that psychologists tend to become more subjectivistic as they get older. This is also certainly possible, though the only evidence that comes to mind consists of a few individual cases. Thus, Abraham Maslow began his career as a disciple of John Watson, and I was a behaviorist myself at 17. In many ways, the objectivistic route is narrower, more restricting, and I can think of others who have followed this route initially and ultimately found it too confining and who have forsaken some of their early methodological vows for the sake of a broader perspective. Examples of the opposite sequence seem more difficult to find, but this matter merits further study.

It would be of interest to know whether there is a systematic relationship between theoretical orientation and professional attainment. Are certain kinds of psychologists more likely to obtain higher degrees or to secure positions of power? There were a number of items included with the TOS items that bear on this. Subjects were asked to indicate the highest academic degrees that they had attained. For purposes of data processing, two points were assigned to this item if the subject had earned a doctorate (Ph.D. or Ed.D.), one point if the highest degree was an M.A. or M.S., and zero points if it was a BA or BS degree. This item yielded significant correlations only with *impersonal causality and quantitative orientation*. These correlations are both positive (.111 and .102 respectively). These factors may reflect a methodological orientation that is conducive to completion of graduate work or one that tends to be instilled in the course of graduate training. There may be some correlation, too, between quantitative orientation and quantitative ability—in which case, the observed correlation may indirectly reflect an ability differential that affects degree attainment.

The attainment of higher degrees obviously is in part a function of professional ambition or striving. Another possible expression of such striving is a tendency to join divisions and societies. (Of course, this type of affiliative behavior can have many other meanings as well.) The specific APA divisions to which an individual belongs are an indication of interest pattern, which is definitely related to theoretical orientation. The number of divisions to which a psychologists belongs, however, appears to be unrelated. It yields near-zero correlations with TOS factors. The same is true for the number of professional societies or associations outside the American Psychological Association to which the subject belongs.

Theoretical orientation proves a bit more related to occupational pursuits. If we dichotomize the total sample into those who are employed in educational institutions and those who are not, we find a slight significant relationship between this dichotomy and factors 3, 4, and I. The academic people tend to have higher scores for *behavioral content emphasis, elementarism,* and *objectivism.* Presumably people in applied areas lean more heavily toward subjectivism, and such people are more numerous in the nonacademic portion of the sample.

Two items were employed to gain a more specific picture of the subject's employment activities. In one item, the subject was asked to characterize his or her primary vocational activity (e.g., teaching, educational administration, research, psychotherapy, personnel selection, vocational guidance, industrial counseling). In the other, the subject was asked to indicate the highest professional position he or she had ever held. The responses to these two items were used in combination as a basis for classifying the subject according to his or her primary activity (at the time of testing or when last employed) in terms of the following seven categories:

1. Clinical work, psychotherapy, psychodiagnostics
2. Teaching
3. Educational administration (including department head, director of counseling service, etc.)
4. Research
5. Counseling or school psychology
6. Industrial work (including business, advertising, mar-

keting, personnel, human engineering, and consulting
with industry, business, and government)
7. Other

It was possible to classify all but seven subjects in terms of the
first six categories. Category 3 was used whenever it was evident
that the subject held an administrative position, even though administrative duties may have consumed less than half of the individual's working time, since the administrative category was of some
interest in its own right. Undoubtedly there are certain personal
qualities that render an individual a more likely candidate for an
administrative position. To judge from present findings, however,
these qualities are quite independent of theoretical orientation.

To assess the relationship between theoretical orientation and
vocational activity, I examined the responses of those subjects who
scored toward the extremes on either of the second-order factors
(*objectivism vs. subjectivism* and *endogenism vs. exogenism*). For each
of these factors, I selected those subjects whose scores lay one
standard deviation or more from the mean. For each of the extreme
groups thus formed, I determined the proportion of subjects falling
into each of the activity categories.

When the extreme groups on factor I are compared, highly significant differences in proportion appear for the categories 1, 2, and 4.
Subjectivists are far more likely than objectivists to be involved in
clinical work. There is a comparable trend for counseling and school
psychology, but the few cases in that category do not yield a significant difference. On the other hand, objectivists are far more likely to
be involved in teaching or research. These differences strongly support the impression that behaviorists tend to be concentrated in
academic facilities, while psychologists at large probably lean more
heavily in a humanistic direction.

When the extreme groups on factor II are compared, only one
significant difference emerges, but it is a very marked difference.
Endogenists are much more likely than exogenists to be engaged
primarily in research. Perhaps some of the research is biological in
character, but probably not enough of it to account for a sharp difference in proportions. It is also possible that people who lean
strongly toward exogenism, being more convinced of the possibilities
of social influence, are more likely to pursue careers in which they
can be effective social agents. This again seems an insufficient explanation of the observed difference. It is possible that temperament
differences between endogenists and exogenists draw them toward

different kinds of careers. We will see other evidence that bears on this.

AREAS OF INTEREST IN PSYCHOLOGY

In one blank on the TOS answer form, the subject was asked to indicate his or her primary area of interest in psychology. The responses were coded in terms of the following 18 categories:

1. Clinical psychology, abnormal psychology, psychotherapy
2. Behavior therapy, behavior analysis, behavior modification
3. Counseling (including academic, vocational, marital, and rehabilitation counseling)
4. Personality
5. Developmental psychology, child psychology
6. Industrial psychology, human factors, industrial organization
7. Educational psychology, school psychology, special education
8. Community psychology
9. Social psychology
10. Learning, conditioning, memory
11. Motivation
12. Physiological psychology, neuropsychology, psychopharmacology
13. Perception, vision, audition, psychophysics
14. Cognition
15. Animal psychology, comparative psychology
16. General experimental psychology
17. Quantitative theory and methods, statistics, measurement, data processing, research design, mathematical psychology
18. Other

High and low groups in the two second-order factors were compared by the same procedure that was applied to the vocational activity data. For the high and low groups on factor I, significant differences appeared for five of the interest categories—categories 1, 2, 5, 10, and 12. The subjectivists more often indicated a primary interest in clinical psychology. There was a similar trend for personality theory, but it was not significant. The objectivists more often gave responses classified as behavior analysis, developmental psychology, learning, or physiological psychology. The second category embraces a variety of activities that are commonly regarded as a part of clinical psychology, but it seemed desirable to use the second category whenever the written response clearly fit that category. Undoubtedly many subjects who simply wrote "clinical psychology" have more specific interests that could place them in the behavior-therapy category. The open-ended item permits only limited discrimination, of course; yet it apparently permits us to distinguish crudely between two very different therapeutic groups, for categories 1 and 2 yield significant differences in opposite directions.

The extreme groups on factor II yield significant differences for categories 2, 3, 5, and 10. Endogenists more often indicated a primary interest in developmental psychology. Exogenists more often indicated an interest in behavior therapy, counseling, and learning. With respect to the most popular interest category, clinical psychology, there was essentially no difference between endogenists and exogenists. There were few subjects who indicated a primary interest in physiological psychology, but these few fell as often into the exogenist group as the endogenist group. This suggests that an interest in biology per se has little to do with the dimension of *endogenism vs. exogenism.*

For a more detailed examination of the relationship between theoretical orientation and interest in various areas of psychology, we can turn to the earlier analysis of the TOS(I) questionnaire. That questionnaire not only called for an indication of the subject's primary area of specialization but also contained a list of 25 areas for which the subject was asked to indicate degree of interest. Hence it provides a basis for determining correlations between interest areas and orientation factors. The 120 orientation items were first subjected to a factor analysis, which yielded 17 obliquely rotated factors. The 25 interest areas were treated as a set of extension variables. The extended factor structure matrix thus provides the correlations between the factors and interest areas.

The interest areas listed in the questionnaire were as follows:

1. Learning and memory
2. Cognitive processes
3. Sensory processes and mechanisms
4. Perception
5. Motivation
6. Animal behavior
7. Physiological psychology

8. Behavior genetics
9. Developmental psychology
10. Psychopathology
11. Psychotherapy and behavior modification
12. Assessment of intellectual and personality variables
13. Personality theory
14. Social interaction and group processes
15. Culture and social systems
16. Attitudes and opinions
17. Language and communication
18. Aesthetics
19. Normal and altered states of consciousness
20. Parapsychology
21. Educational psychology
22. Personnel and industrial psychology
23. The history of psychology
24. Philosophical issues in psychology
25. Statistical methods

Table 6 shows the correlations between these interest areas and eight factors of theoretical orientation. To facilitate comparison of these results with the others that we will consider in the remaining chapters, I have extracted from the TOS(I) analysis those factors that correspond to the scales of the final version of the Theoretical Orientation Survey. I have also reflected two columns of correlations, so that the eight factors all conform in direction to the eight TOS factors. Thus, they represent the following eight dimensions:

1. Factual (vs. theoretical) orientation
2. Impersonal causality (vs. personal will)
3. Behavioral (vs. experiential) content emphasis
4. Elementarism (vs. holism)
5. Biological determinism
6. Environmental determinism
7. Physicalism
8. Quantitative (vs. qualitative) orientation

As we examine the correlations, it is useful to remember that factors 5 and 6 are the main components of the second-order factor of *endogenism vs. exogenism* and are oppositely loaded by it. The remaining factors may all be regarded as components of the second-order factor of *objectivism vs. subjectivism,* though *quantitative orientation* was only weakly loaded by this in the TOS(I) analysis and *factual orientation* was rather weakly loaded in the TOS(II) analysis. We may note, too, that since these correlations are based on the responses of 299 subjects, most of the values we see in the table are statistically significant, though not necessarily large enough to be very meaningful.

In this table, the components of *objectivism vs. subjectivism* tend to display rather similar patterns of correlation. In fact, we can summarize much of the information in the table by listing some 15 interest variables with which those factors correlate in much the same way. Thus, the components of *objectivism (factual orientation, impersonal causality, behavioral content emphasis, elementarism, physicalism,* and *quantitative orientation)* correlate positively with variables 1 (learning and memory) and 6 (animal behavior). They correlate negatively with variables 2 (cognitive processes), 9 (developmental psychology,) 10 (psychopathology), 11 (psychotherapy and behavior modification), 12 (assessment of intellectual and personality variables), 13 (personality theory), 14 (social interaction and group processes), 15 (culture and social systems), 16 (attitudes and opinions), 17 (language and communication), 18 (aesthetics), 19 (normal and altered states of consciousness), and 20 (parapsychology). The correlations tend to run highest for the factor of *behavioral content emphasis,* perhaps the most central ingredient in the second-order factor of *objectivism.* They most often drop to a low level for the more peripheral components of *quantitative orientation* and *factual orientation.*

If we want to consider lower correlational values, there are other variables we can add to the list. Thus, the components of *objectivism* tend to correlate positively with an interest in physiological psychology (variable 7) and negatively with interests in perception (4) and educational psychology (21). Perhaps the most striking thing about this total picture is the prevalence of negative correlations. People who score high on the components of *objectivism* tend to display a relatively low interest in some of the areas listed, including many quite traditional areas of psychological subject matter. There are probably two main ways in which we might interpret this finding. For one thing, the concern of the objectivist for "objective" methods and subject matter may simply lead him to reject areas of study in which investigators are likely to focus in any way on the conscious experience of the individual. Relatively "safe" areas would include learning, animal behavior, and physiological psychology. Other traditional areas of experimentation, as well as the broad domains of clinical psychology, personality theory, social psychology, and developmental psychology are more problematical for anyone who expouses a very strict methodological behaviorism.

Another possible interpretation is that objectivists tend to have more sharply focused interests. Thus the objectivist may tend to become a specialist or authority in one narrow area and may devote a career to the study of serial learning, the galvanic skin response, or dominance behavior in chickens. Such an exclusive focus may lead the objectivist to see a relatively large number of areas as peripheral or foreign to his interests—including areas in which other objectivists specialize. Even the broadest, most poorly circumscribed areas on the list may be seen as containing nothing to which he wishes to devote his attention. The subjectivist, in contrast, presumably has more fluid and wide-ranging interests. To the extent that he conforms to my picture of the "fluid" type, he can tolerate looser methodology and he can more readily tolerate the unanalyzable full complexity of human behavior and experience.

Turning to the components of *endogenism vs. exogenism*, we find that these apparently bear much less relationship to areas of interest in psychology. In the fifth column of correlations, there is no value greater than .21, and in the sixth column none above .18. If we consider the correlations at a level of .15 and above, we can see that *biological determinism* tends to be related positively to interests in cognitive processes (variable 2), sensory processes and mechanisms (3), animal behavior (6), physiological psychology (7), and behavior genetics (8) and related negatively to psychopathology (10) and social interaction and group processes (14). *Environmental determinism* tends to relate negatively to interests in esthetics (18), normal and altered states of consciousness (19) and parapsychology (20). It is clearly possible to make some sense of these correlations, but clearly the main lesson of these data is that *endogenism* and its components are pretty independent of subject matter interests in psychology. At least this is true when we are dealing with the questionnaire factors identified as *biological determinism, environmental determinism,* and *endogenism*. The factor of *endogenism vs. exogenism* which I originally found in the analysis of theorist ratings may have been more of a subject-matter dimension.

We have considered the data for only eight factors here, and we might note what the extended factor structure matrix reveals with respect to the other nine factors of the TOS(I) analysis. The ones that most clearly manifest distinctive patterns of correlations are those that I labeled *humanism vs. scientific detachment, emphasis on phylogenetic continuity* (vs. emphasis on human distinctiveness), and *physiological reductionism*. All three of these factors were found in the TOS(I) analysis to be loaded substantially by *objectivism vs. subjectivism*. Thus, it is not surprising that they manifest high correlations with essentially the same interest areas as do the components of *objectivism* that we have already considered. For *emphasis on phylogenetic continuity* and *physiological reductionism,* the sign pattern is the same as that which we noted above for *factual orientation, impersonal causality, behavioral content emphasis, elementarism, physicalism,* and *quantitative orientation.* For the factor of *humanism vs. scientific detachment,* the sign pattern is reversed, since in that factor the positive pole is subjectivistic. For the remaining six factors, the correlations are generally low.

Perhaps we should add a few observations regarding some of the variables that have thus far escaped mention. Motivation (variable 5) most strongly attracts people who are theoretically oriented (low on factor 1), but its correlations are altogether quite low. It is a broad area of basic theory that necessarily demands the attention of psychologists of various orientations (who deal with it in various ways). The history of psychology (variable 23) also draws the interest of many kinds of psychologists. The near-zero correlations yielded by this variable suggest that the history specialists who served as judges in my rating research may have been a fairly unbiased sample with respect to theoretical orientation. Variable 24, philosophical issues in psychology, shows a slight tendency to fit the subjectivism pattern—the pattern of those variables that correlate negatively with the components of *objectivism.* Its highest correlation, not shown in the table, is with the factor of *humanism* (.28). An interest in statistical methods, variable 25, yields only one correlation of appreciable size—not too surprisingly, with *quantitative orientation.*

The factors of the TOS(I) analysis were also related to the subjects' primary fields of specialization in psychology. For this purpose, I classified subjects in terms of the following categories. For each category, I have indicated in parentheses the number of subjects so classified:

1. Clinical psychology, psychotherapy, psychopathology (43)
2. Social psychology, psycholinguistics, attitudes, organizational behavior, psychology of religion (38)
3. Learning, memory, motivation (31)
4. Perception, sensation, psychophysics, vision, acoustics, (19)
5. Physiological psychology, behavior genetics, psychopharmacology (15)
6. General experimental psychology, animal psychology, comparative psychology, behavior theory, mathematical psychology (24)
7. Cognition, cognitive processes, thinking (10)

8. Developmental psychology, child psychology (15)

9. Quantitative methods, statistics, measurement, research design, differential psychology, psychological tests (9)

10. Industrial psychology, personnel psychology, management psychology, human engineering, human factors (12)

11. Counseling, guidance (18)

12. Educational psychology, school psychology (16)

13. Personality theory, personality measurement (11)

14. History, systems, theoretical psychology, philosophical psychology (4)

15. No response or nonspecific response (34)

These categories, like those mentioned earlier, represent an attempt to accommodate the responses actually given by subjects. Most of these categories can be aligned with those employed in the analysis described earlier in this section, but there are some obvious minor differences.

For the purpose of this analysis, I first grouped subjects according to area of specialization, and for each of the resulting groups I determined the mean and standard deviation on each of the TOS(I) factors. In a sense, this is the reverse of the procedure I described above for the TOS data, and it provides a more direct picture of the characteristics of the people in each specialty area. With respect to its overall implications, this procedure yields essentially the same picture as the one provided by the procedures already discussed, with perhaps a few more details added. In the present case, I compared the data for each of the specialty subgroups with the corresponding data for the remainder of the total sample. For each subgroup, I identified those factors on which it deviated significantly from the rest of the sample (i.e., those factors on which its mean differed by an amount exceeding the 5% level of significance). Since most of the subgroups are rather small, I will confine my attention in the descriptions below to the information yielded by these significant deviations. To simplify description, I will characterize each group in terms of the pole of any given factor toward which its scores tend to deviate. For example, I will say that the group tends toward impersonal causality if it has a significantly high mean on factor 2, but toward personal will if it has a significantly low mean on that factor.

There are two groups, specialists in learning and physiological psychology, who display an overall pattern that can clearly be characterized as objectivistic. In both of these groups, we find significant trends toward factual orientation, behavior content emphasis, elementarism, scientific detachment, and emphasis on phylogenetic continuity. In addition, the learning specialists display an emphasis on impersonal causality, physicalism, and absence of psychophysical dualism. Additional features of the physiological psychology group include physiological reductionism and emphasis on physiological correlates.

Two groups that display some tendency toward the objectivistic pattern are the specialists in perception and the specialists in general experimental psychology. The significant features of the perception group are scientific detachment, physiological reductionism, emphasis on physiological correlates, and advocacy of physical theoretical models. In the general experimental psychology group, we find behavioral content emphasis, biological determinism, scientific detachment, emphasis on phylogenetic continuity, quantitative orientation, and advocacy of physical theoretical models. We might expect the specialists in quantitative methods also to fit the objectivistic pattern, but their only significant feature is quantitative orientation. Apart from this, they show no clear tendency (in their nonsignificant deviations) to fit either an objectivistic or a subjectivistic pattern.

The groups that display patterns that can best be characterized as subjectivistic are the clinical and counseling groups. In both of these groups, we find theoretical (rather than factual) orientation, personal will, experiential content emphasis, holism, low biological determinism, humanism, emphasis on human distinctiveness, low physicalism, low physiological reductionism, low emphasis on physiological correlates, and rejection of physical theoretical models. Additional significant features in the clinical group are qualitative orientation and low systematism. One additional feature in the counseling group is psychophysical dualism.

The educational psychology and personality groups show patterns that resemble those of the clinical and counseling groups, but they yield fewer significant mean values. The only significant feature for the educational psychology group is low biological determinism; for the components of *objectivism vs. subjectivism,* there are merely nonsignificant trends in the subjectivistic direction. For the personality group the significant features are limited to biological determinism, low environmental determinism, emphasis on human distinctiveness, and low physicalism.

It may be noted that with the combination of biological determinism and low environmental determinism, the personality group comes closest to fitting an endogenist pattern. [In the TOS(I) analysis, the low physicalism is also part of this pattern.] The only other group that shows a significant trend toward either of these features is the general experimental group. I have noted three groups that display the opposite trend (low mean) for biological determinism—the clinical, counseling, and educational psychology groups. The full exogenist pattern (low biological determinism, high environmental determinism) is found in one group—the industrial psychologists. The one additional feature that is significant for this group is psychophysical dualism.

The four remaining groups appear not to be very distinctive. The one significant feature in the social psychology group is an emphasis on human distinctiveness. For the cognition and developmental psychology groups, there are no significant features. For the history group, which contains only four people, we find an emphasis on unconscious motivation and low explicit conceptualization. In the research I have done so far, the examination of specialty groups has been a rather peripheral concern. Perhaps this matter is worthy of more direct study with larger groups.

ALLIANCE WITH PROMINENT THEORISTS

In one of the blanks on the TOS answer form, the subject was asked to write the name of the prominent theorist whose views on theoretical issues corresponded most closely to the subject's own views. In the preceding chapter, we considered the results obtained by tallying the responses (and nonresponses) of 866 subjects. Perhaps the relationship of these responses to theoretical orientation is fairly obvious, but it is sometimes important to examine obvious relationships. As we will see, the relationships found with the TOS agree very well with those revealed by a related examination of TOS(II) data, which we considered in Chapter 3.

As I noted earlier in the chapter, I had identified those subjects who scored either very high or very low on either of the two second-order factors for which the TOS is scored. I compared these extreme groups with respect to the frequency with which they named any of 12 different theorists. The 12 theorists were those named most often by the total sample:

1. Alfred Adler
2. Gordon W. Allport
3. Erik Erikson

4. Sigmund Freud
5. Carl G. Jung
6. Kurt Lewin
7. Abraham Maslow
8. Frederick Perls
9. Jean Piaget
10. Carl Rogers
11. B. F. Skinner
12. H. S. Sullivan

There were significant differences between the two extreme groups on the first second-order factor for seven theorists. The one theorist mentioned much more often—indeed, exclusively—by the objectivists was B. F. Skinner. The theorists mentioned significantly more often by the subjectivists were Erikson, Freud, Jung, Maslow, Perls, and Sullivan. Adler, Allport, and Rogers obviously belong in this cluster, but they were named too infrequently to yield significant differences.

For the extreme groups on the second factor, there are significant differences for six theorists. Erikson, Freud, Jung, and Piaget were all named more often by the endogenists. One ingredient that is common to the theoretical systems of these four is the idea of a natural developmental process. The only other theorist in the list who shows a comparable concern with developmental stages is Sullivan, who places more emphasis on the effects of social interaction. There are two theorists who are strongly favored by the exogenist subjects—Rogers and Skinner. This seems an interesting combination in view of the opposing views of these two men on issues relating to the objectivism-subjectivism dimension. Perhaps with respect to *endogenism vs. exogenism,* they share a bit of common ground, but Skinner is known for a rather extreme position with respect to environmental determinism, and Rogers is not. As I suggested before, of course, both of these theorists may be favored by psychologists who have a practical interest in being effective social agents.

PSYCHOTHERAPEUTIC ORIENTATION

While Rogers and Skinner share an interest in methods for producing desired social effects, they represent much different views regarding the proper course for achieving effects, and their differences are mirrored in divisions that we find today within the profession of clinical psychology. In one of the analyses I reported earlier in this chapter, these differences were reflected to some degree in the contrasting outlooks of specialty groups identified as "clinical psychology" and "behavior therapy." There has been one study designed specifically to relate the factors of theoretical orientation to views on the therapeutic process.

In the course of research for a doctoral dissertation, Linda Wyrick developed a Therapy Orientation Survey.[11] This instrument contained 50 Likert items and was designed in such a way that high scores indicated an inclination to become personally or emotionally involved with patients and to regard personal involvement as desirable. Low scores represented a tendency to avoid personal involvement with patients and to favor the maintenance of personal distance as a feature of sound therapeutic strategy. The Therapy Orientation Survey and TOS(I) were mailed together to 500 correspondents who were identified from APA Directory entries as clinical psychologists.

The correspondents were asked to complete both questionnaires and to indicate which of three basic approaches to therapy they favored most strongly—analytic therapy, behavior therapy, or experiential therapy. Subjects who failed to select one of these categories, i.e., subjects who marked a combination of them or wrote in an alternative designation, were treated as an "eclectic" group for purposes of data processing. Returns were received from 133 individuals.

The score on the Therapy Orientation Survey discriminated significantly among the four therapist groups. In terms of descending mean scores, the four groups ran as follows: analytic therapists (179.851), experiential therapists (179.257), eclectic therapists (172.533), and behavior therapists (162.619). There is no significant difference between the first two groups, but these both differ sharply from the behavior therapists, while the eclectic group is intermediate. Assuming that Freud is the predominant influence in the first group, its high mean may seem a bit surprising in view of Freud's insistence on playing the role of an opaque observer. Of course, Freud himself did not always adhere rigidly to his own rule. Furthermore, he did recognize that the therapist will tend to respond emotionally to his patient and that he must be prepared to do a good deal of self-analysis to cope with his countertransference. Thus, therapists of Freudian persuasion have always recognized personal involvement with patients, at least in some form, as a fact of life. Moreover, most of them as individuals are less austere than Freud himself. The fact that analytic and experiential therapists in combination differ markedly from behavior therapists on the Therapy Orientation Survey suggests that the sort of personal involvement assessed by this scale is closely related to subjectivism.

Obviously we can best evaluate this relationship by examining correlations between the two instruments that were mailed to the correspondents. For all subjects, scores were computed for all 17 factors yielded by the analysis of TOS(I), and these scores were correlated with those for the Therapy Orientation Survey. Below I have listed the 17 factors, identifying each in terms of the positive or high-scoring end as yielded by the TOS(I) analysis, and indicated their respective correlations with personal involvement:

1. Factual (vs. theoretical) orientation: −.335
2. Impersonal causality (vs. personal will): −.275
3. Experiential (vs. behavioral) content emphasis: .600
4. Holism (vs. elementarism): .542
5. Biological determinism: −.050
6. Social determinism: −.213
7. Humanism (vs. scientific detachment): .302
8. Emphasis on phylogenetic continuity (vs. emphasis on human distinctiveness): −.451
9. Physicalism: −.368
10. Emphasis on unconscious motivation (vs. emphasis on conscious motivation): .343
11. Systematism: −.325
12. Quantitative (vs. qualitative) orientation: −.193
13. Physiological reductionism: −.345
14. Emphasis on physiological correlates: .198
15. Rejection (vs. advocacy) of physical theoretical models: .006
16. Explicit conceptualization: −.127
17. Psychophysical dualism: .018

These correlations are all statistically significant, with the exception of those for factors 5, 15, 16, and 17. All the factors that are loaded substantially by the second-order factor of *objectivism vs. subjectivism* in the TOS(I) analysis—factors 1, 2, 3, 4, 7, 8, and 9—correlate well with personal involvement, and they tend to correlate more highly than do the remaining factors. The directions of these correlations are such that personal involvement goes in each case with the subjectivistic pole of the factor. The association is particularly marked for experiential content emphasis and holism. Thus, the therapist who favors personal involvement with patients favors more concern in theory with the total experiencing person.

The four therapist groups were compared with respect to theoretical orientation scores. As we would expect from their scores on personal involvement, the analytic and experiential groups tended to score similarly and tended both to differ from the behavior therapist group. In most cases, however, the experiential therapists differed from the behavior therapists more than the analytic therapists did. F tests revealed significant group differences for 13 of the factors, and for all but three of these the experiential therapists and behavior therapists are the two extreme groups.

For seven factors—factors 1, 2, 6, 8, 9, 11, and 12—the four group means follow the same pattern. From high to low in terms of mean score, the groups run as follows: behavior therapists, eclectic therapists, analytic therapists, experiential therapists. For two other factors—factors 3 and 4—we find just the reverse pattern: experiential therapists, followed by analytic therapists, then eclectic therapists, and then behavior therapists. In terms of the relative characteristics of the extreme groups, this means that behavior therapists tend toward factual orientation, impersonal causality, behavioral content emphasis, elementarism, social determinism, emphasis on phylogenetic continuity, physicalism, systematism, and quantitative orientation. In contrast, experiential therapists tend toward theoretical orientation, personal will, experiential content emphasis, holism, low social determinism, emphasis on human distinctiveness, low physicalism, low systematism, and qualitative orientation. This description encompasses most of the components of *subjectivism vs. objectivism,* and we can summarize most of it by saying that behavior therapists tends to be objectivistic, while experiential therapists tend to be subjectivistic. The other two groups fall between, with the analytic therapists tending to resemble the experiential therapists.

Factor 13 shows nearly the same pattern, but the extreme groups are the behavior therapists (who tend toward physiological reductionism) and the analytic therapists (who score lowest). The difference between the experiential and analytic therapists, however, is small and insignificant. The one component of *subjectivism vs. objectivism* that shows a rather deviant pattern is factor 7, where the groups run in the order experiential, eclectic, analytic, and behavior therapy. Here the experiential therapists lean most strongly toward humanism, while the analytic therapists resemble the behavior therapists in scoring toward the scientific-detachment end of the factor. Perhaps this is the one measured variable that reflects the Freudian prescription of therapeutic aloofness.

Two other factors show significant group differences. On factor 10, the analytic therapists score highest, followed by the eclectic therapists, experiential therapists, and behavior therapists. As we would expect, unconscious motivation is stressed most heavily by the analytic therapists. The behavior therapists are most likely to reject the concept, while the experiential therapists place more emphasis on conscious experience. On factor 16, the order from high to low is eclectic therapists, analytic therapists, behavior therapists, and experiential therapists. This is difficult to interpret, since the eclectics score most distinctively (they differ from the other groups more than those groups differ from one another), and they are an ill-defined entity. For the other three groups, this might be the order we would expect with regard to relative emphasis on formal theory.

6. Life-History Variables

In this chapter and the two that follow we will be concerned with the information provided by the battery of instruments sent to various portions of the TOS research sample. As I noted in Chapter 5, this battery was divided into four parts or packages, and each of these was sent to a different subsample. We will consider first the information on life-history variables provided by the biographical questionnaire and the Roe-Siegelman Parent-Child Relations Questionnaire. These two instruments were in the same package, and they were both completed by a total of 158 subjects, including 75 men and 83 women. I had sought a somewhat larger sample for these instuments than for the other ones in the battery, because they encompass many variables that demand separate consideration of male and female subjects. In the descriptions presented in the pages that follow, I will note sex differences wherever they are evident; where I do not mention them, it may be assumed that essentially the same trend is found for men and women. The present instruments also encompass a wide array of variables that are difficult to measure reliably. On the whole, they yield few sizable correlations with the theoretical orientation factors, compared with the variables we will consider later. If we want to understand the determinants of theoretical orientation, however, it may be as important to know what kinds of experiences do not affect it as to know what kinds do.

It must be recognized that this investigation of life-history variables is basically an exploratory operation. There was little basis for predicting relationships between the variables in this realm and theoretical orientation. Since I dealt with a large number of variables here, it was inevitable that many of them would yield significant values, i.e., correlation coefficients, t ratios, or Chi-squares of a magnitude that would be expected no more than 5 percent of the time by chance. Many of these significant values would not prove replicable if the study were repeated. We can attach greater importance to them, however, when the value is not merely significant but large (hence very highly significant), where the same trend occurs in both sexes, and where there is a consistent pattern involving all first-order components of a second-order factor.

FAMILY DEMOGRAPHIC CHARACTERISTICS AND RELIGION

The place of birth of the subject was coded in terms of seven regions: (1) New England states, (2) Middle Atlantic states, (3) Southern states, (4) Central states, (5) Mountain states, (6) Pacific states, and (7) foreign countries and United States territories. The only region that appeared to be related to theoretical orientation was the second, which was coded much more often for subjectivistic subjects, particularly subjectivistic female subjects. The second category includes the states of New York, New Jersey, Pennsylvania, Delaware, Maryland, and West Virginia, as well as Washington, D.C. The category is a bit misleading, however, for in a large percentage of cases, the birthplace was more specifically New York City. When we examine the evidence for birthplace of parents, we find a slight tendency for foreign birth for either parent to be associated with the components of subjectivism. Perhaps both of these pieces of information imply that subjectivists are a little less likely than objectivists to be products of Middle America and more likely to have a cosmopolitan background that includes some elements of continental European culture.

The biographical questionnaire included questions pertaining to the education and occupations of the parents. There was no discernible relationship between theoretical orientation and the amount of the education of either parent, the occupational level of either parent, the field of either parent's occupation, or the tendency for the mother to have been employed outside the home. Family size (number of siblings) and order of birth within the family also appeared to have little bearing on theoretical orientation.

Religion appeared to be somewhat more important. Subjectivists showed a significantly greater tendency than objectivists to regard religion as personally important. The components of *objectivism* all correlated negatively with personal importance of religion, and these correlations were significant for *impersonal causality, behavioral content emphasis,* and *physicalism.* Subjectivists were also more likely to indicate that religion was important to their parents. This trend was significant for the fathers of male subjects, the mothers of female subjects, and for the mothers of all subjects combined. Again corresponding trends were found for the components of *objectivism vs. subjectivism,* and several of these were significant. (For example, for the total sample, importance of religion for the mother had significant negative correlations with *behavioral content emphasis, elementarism, physicalism,* and *quantitative orientation.*)

Church attendance was clearly less pertinent than religion. The church attendance of the subject was essentially unrelated to theoretical orientation. The church attendance of the father and the church attendance of the mother had weak but significant negative correlations with *quantitative orientation,* but were otherwise inconsequential.

The specific character of the individual's religious beliefs or affiliation appeared to be of some importance, but of less importance than religion per se. Apparently the tendency to subscribe to some specifiable religion (not to respond with "none," "atheist," or "agnostic") goes with subjectivism. Its correlation with *objectivism vs. subjectivism* is −.271 for the total sample, −.348 for men, and −.227 for women. It also correlates negatively with all the components of objectivism, and for the total sample these correlations are significant for *impersonal causality, behavioral content emphasis, elementarism,* and *physicalism.* The tendency to agree with the parents with respect to basic religious commitment, on the other hand, appears to be less important. It yielded only one significant correlation (−.224 with *elementarism* for the female subjects).

Religious affiliation was coded in terms of nine categories: (1) none, atheist, agnostic; (2) Jewish; (3) Roman Catholic, Greek Orthodox, Russian Orthodox; (4) Protestant denominations without central church control (Congregational, Quaker, Unitarian, Universalist); (5) major centralized Protestant denominations (Presbyterian, Baptist, Methodist, etc.); (6) evangelical Protestant denominations (Southern Baptist, Lutheran, Mormon, Disciples of Christ, etc.); (7) Christian Science and other healing churches; (8) Oriental; (9) other. The first category, of course, tended to be associated with objectivism. The only other category which yielded a significant relationship was the second. Subjects who scored toward the subjectivist end of the second-order dimension were more likely than the objectivists to be Jewish. This association, however, barely reached the 5 percent level of significance. There were comparable trends for an association between subjectivism and Jewish religion for father and for mother, but these trends fell short of statistical significance. On the other hand, objectivism was significantly associated with a lack of religious affiliation on the part of the mother for the total sample, and for men it was associated with a lack of religious affiliation on the part of either parent.

Apparently religion has much less to do with the other second-order factor, *endogenism vs. exogenism,* and its components, for this factor appears to be unrelated to the importance-of-religion and church-attendance variables. For some reason, however, there is a significantly greater tendency for endogenists, as compared to exogenists, to give denominational responses that fit the fourth category (Congregational, Quaker, Unitarian, Universalist). For most of these subjects this affiliation represents an independent choice of a "liberal" Protestant church, for there were very few parents belonging to any of these denominations. But it is not clear why such a choice should be characteristic of endogenists—if further research should indicate that, indeed, it is.

Conceivably the greater emphasis on religion of the subjectivists could point to greater conservatism or conventionality, although the insignificance of church attendance does not support this idea. Furthermore, radicalism-conservativism in the political realm shows no relationship to theoretical orientation for the total sample. The one significant correlation for the item in which subjects were asked to indicate the degree of radicalism (vs. conservatism) of their political views is a negative correlation with *elementarism* for women—which would align conservatism with the objectivist end of that factor. Agreement with parents with respect to party preference also shows little relationship in general to theoretical orientation, but it does show a small negative correlation with *biological orientation* for men.

The socioeconomic status of the family evidently has nothing to do with theoretical orientation. I have noted two relevant variables—education and occupational level of parents. A third relevant variable, the financial position of the family during the subject's childhood and adolescence, also yields correlations close to zero.

RELATIONSHIPS WITH PARENTS

The biographical questionnaire contained items pertaining to parental divorce and to separation of the subject from the parents, by divorce or death, during childhood and adolescence. Parental death and divorce yielded nothing significant, but there was a tendency, significant for women and for the total sample, for subjects high on *elementarism* to have lived mainly with just one or with neither parent.

There were four items that yielded a score for mother vs. father domination of the household. This yielded nothing significant. The closeness of the subject to either or both parents appeared to be more important. There were three items that yielded a score for "interaction balance." A high score represented greater relative closeness to the mother, while a low score represented greater relative closeness to the father. For the women, this related negatively with *objectivism* (and similarly with the first-order factors of *behavioral content emphasis* and *elementarism*) and positively with *endogenism* (with supporting positive and negative correlations respectively with *biological determinism* and *environmental determinism*). These trends were not found for the men, and for the total sample only the positive correlation with *biological determinism* was significant. For the men, there was a significant positive correlation with *impersonal causality*. The most consistent pattern here, however, points to a tendency for women who were relatively closer to their mothers to be subjectivistic and endogenist.

There were three additional items that yielded a score for closeness to father (not treated relatively) and three items that yielded a score for closeness to mother. For these variables, nearly all the significant correlations were negative correlations with *objectivism* and its components. For the men, closeness to father correlated negatively with *behavioral content emphasis, physicalism,* and *objectivism*. Closeness to mother yielded no significant correlations. For the women, closeness to father correlated negatively with *factual orientation*. Closeness to mother correlated negatively with *impersonal causality, elementarism, physicalism,* and *objectivism*. For the total sample, closeness to father correlated negatively with *factual orientation, behavioral content emphasis, physicalism,* and *objectivism*. Closeness to mother correlated negatively with *elementarism* and *objectivism*. The only significant correlation that runs counter to the total pattern is a positive correlation for women between closeness to father and *quantitative orientation*. It is possible that in women an interest in the mathematical realm in particular is often fostered by a close relationship and perhaps identification with the father.

The implication of this total pattern is that subjectivists are more likely to have had close and harmonious relationships with their parents. The objectivist is a little more likely to have been at odds with a parent, particularly the parent of the same sex. Subjects were also asked to what extent they perceived the behavior of their parents toward them as consistent or inconsistent, and the consistency items yield the same sort of picture as the closeness items. Thus, for men, consistency of father correlates negatively with *factual orientation, impersonal causality, behavioral content emphasis, physicalism,* and *objectivism*, while consistency of mother yields no significant correlations. For women, consistency of father yields no significant correlations, but consistency of mother correlates negatively with *elementarism, physicalism,* and *objectivism.* For the total sample, there are just two significant correlations—father's consistency correlates negatively with *factual orientation* and *impersonal causality.* The overall trend, then is for the objectivist to regard the parent of the same sex as having been inconsistent in the imposition of rules and in the meting out of rewards and punishments.

There were items pertaining to friction among the adults (which would usually mean between parents) and among the children in the family in which the subject grew up. The friction-among-children item yielded nothing significant. Friction among adults yielded one significant correlation—a negative correlation for women with *behavioral content emphasis.* This suggests that the mother who clashed with the subject was also seen as clashing with the father, but the overall correlation pattern for the friction-among-adults item is not impressive.

The remaining family interaction items in the biographical questionnaire pertained to parental pressure in the choice of a career. Here the few significant correlations seemed to involve the parent of the opposite sex. For men, maternal pressure correlated positively with *biological orientation.* For women, paternal pressure correlated positively with *impersonal causality* and *objectivism.* The only significant correlation for the total sample was a positive correlation between paternal pressure and *impersonal causality.* The correlations for the female subjects are the highest and suggest that objectivism in women may be associated with paternal pressure to pursue a "masculine" career (objectivism itself being correlated with a preference for traditionally masculine careers).

The Roe-Siegelman Parent-Child Relations Questionnaire provides information closely related to that which we have just considered. In this questionnaire, the subject marks items pertaining to many different aspects of parental behavior which he or she experienced as a child. There are four separate forms for the questionnaire—a male form for fathers, a male form for mothers, a female form for fathers, and a female form for mothers. Each of these yields scores for five basic parent-behavior variables: loving, demanding, attentive, rejecting, and casual. In addition, a factor score for loving-rejecting is obtained by subtracting the rejecting score from the loving score, and a factor score for casual-demanding is obtained by subtracting the demanding score from the casual score. The latter scores correspond to the two dimensions that have most often appeared in factor analyses of parental attitudes and behavior—a dimension of love or acceptance (vs. rejection) and a dimension of control (vs. permissiveness or casualness).

The correlations between the PCR variables and the TOS factors are shown in Tables 7 and 8. We might expect the loving and rejecting variables to correspond most closely to the closeness variable of the biographical questionnaire. Indeed, correlations between biographical-questionnaire and PCR variables clearly bear out this expectation. For the men, closeness to mother correlates .760 with love from the mother, −.644 with rejection from the mother, and .735 with the loving-rejecting factor. For the women, the corresponding values are .544, −.549, and .565. For males, closeness to father correlates .725 with love from the father, −.711 with rejection from the father, and .764 with the loving-rejecting factor. The corresponding values for the female subsample are .703, −.646, and .705. Given this correspondence we might expect *objectivism* to correlate negatively with love and loving-rejecting for the parent of the same sex. For women, none of the pertinent correlations are significant. For men, the only significant correlations that accord with this expectation are positive correlations between paternal rejection and *factual orientation* and between paternal rejection and *physicalism* and a negative correlation between the loving-rejecting factor for the father and *physicalism*. Perhaps there are other important elements in closeness that are not captured by the PCR factors.

Love and rejection from the mother yield no significant TOS correlations for either sex. For women, father's love and loving-rejecting yield significant positive correlations with *quantitative orientation*. This is consistent with our finding for *quantitative orientation* and closeness.

The bulk of the significant correlations with the PCR point, however, to a somewhat different kind of pattern—a tendency for *objectivism* and its components to be associated with a controlling father. For men, the demanding father variable correlates positively with *behavioral content emphasis, physicalism,* and *objectivism*. For women, it correlates positively with *factual orientation* and *impersonal causality*. For men, the casual father variable correlates negatively with *behavioral content emphasis, quantitative orientation,* and *objectivism*. For women, it correlates negatively with *factual orientation*. For men, the casual-demanding factor for fathers correlates negatively with *behavioral content emphasis, physicalism, quantitative orientation,* and *objectivism*. For women, it correlates negatively with *factual orientation, impersonal causality,* and *objectivism*. We have a very consistent pattern here, for of the remaining, insignificant correlations, the only one that conflicts with it is a correlation of .005 between casual father and *factual orientation* for men—for all practical purposes, a zero correlation with a rather peripheral component of *objectivism.*

Thus, in general it appears that objectivists of either sex are more likely to have had relatively demanding or controlling fathers, while subjectivists are more likely to have had rather casual, permissive fathers. Apart from a slight trend for female subjects, there is nothing comparable with respect to maternal behavior. (For the women, demanding mother correlates positively with *impersonal causality* and *elementarism,* while the casual-demanding factor for mothers correlates negatively with *elementarism.*) A possible way of construing the general pattern here is in terms of a certain kind of conventionality—the objectivists come from homes in which the father adheres rather strictly to a traditional paternal role expectation. Perhaps a more plausible line of interpretation is one in terms of control per se. The objectivist is interested in a certain kind of control—he seeks precision, he restricts his focus, and he attends to the concrete in an effort to achieve order and avoid uncertainty. Perhaps the main implication of present findings is that such an individual is likely to have been subjected to a relatively great amount of control as a child, particularly from the father. The subjectivist experienced less restriction as a child and possibly for this reason developed a greater tolerance for disorder or a weaker need for order.

The PCR variables show little relationship to *endogenism* and its components. There are only two significant correlations. For men, maternal attention correlates positively with *biological determinism* and *endogenism.* Actually there is a consistent sign pattern for the attention variable for both sexes and both parents—positive correlations with factors 5 and II, negative correlations with factor 6. The attention variable of the PCR was formerly characterized as protection, and many of the scale items suggest a kind of parental indulgence. Other evidence indicates that the endogenists tended as children to be less physically active and aggressive than the exogenists, to have been more inclined toward "flight" than "fight." It is easy to think of parental indulgence and protection as either a consequence or a determinant of such a disposition.

CHILDHOOD EXPERIENCES

The social experiences of childhood undoubtedly have some influence on adult personality and on the choice of a career. There were several items in the biographical questionnaire pertaining to social experiences of various kinds—adult entertaining in the home, visits by other children in the home, number of childhood friends, and amount of time spent in solitary pursuits. The weights assigned to the various answers to these items were summed to provide a total score for childhood experiences of social activities. This yielded no significant correlations with TOS factors. Before I processed any data, however, I had suspected that the items pertaining to childhood friends and to solitary activities might be the ones most indicative of basic temperament and that important information might be obscured by the total score; so I computed correlation coefficients using those specific items. The amount of time spent in solitary pursuits yielded nothing significant. The number of friends which the subject had at most times during childhood, however, yielded a number of significant values and appeared to be related to both objectivism and exogenism. For the total sample, it correlated positively with *factual orientation, elementarism,* and *environmental determinism,* and negatively with *endogenism vs. exogenism.* There were no significant correlations for the male subsample, however, and the trends found in the total sample were almost entirely dependent on covariation among the female subjects. For the women, number of childhood friends correlated with *behavioral content emphasis* (.220), *elementarism* (.241), *environmental determinism* (.350), *physicalism* (.227), *objectivism* (.230), and *endogenism* (−.243).

In certain senses, both objectivism and exogenism imply a kind of "extraverted" orientation—in one case, a focus on the externally observable and in the other case a focus on external determinants. This is the first bit of evidence that suggests that social extraversion may be part of the same package. Further evidence is found in a tendency for shyness in childhood to be reported a little more often by subjectivists and endogenists. In the total sample, shyness correlates negatively with *behavioral content emphasis* and *environmental determinism* and positively with *endogenism.* For men, it correlates negatively with *factual orientation.* For women, it correlates negatively with *behavioral content emphasis, environmental determinism,* and *quantitative orientation.* If we think of the dimension of *objectivism vs. subjectivism* as a manifestation within psychology of a polarity of outlook that distinguishes the natural sciences from the humanities, the present findings run counter to the findings of Roe and Galinsky that I cited in Chapter 2. Their evidence indicates that shyness and social isolation in childhood are found more often in the life histories of physicists and biologists than in those of social scientists (who are presumably midway between the natural sciences and the humanities).

Shyness was one of the ingredients of an item in which subjects were asked to check those problems they had had as children. The problems listed included shyness, frequent fights, strong fears, frequent or chronic illness, sensory or motor handicap, and difficulties (clashes) with teachers. The item was scored dichotomously for each of these problem areas as well as scored for the total number of problems checked. The correlations between these scores and the TOS factors are shown in Table 9. The problem area that correlates best with *objectivism vs. subjectivism* and its components is sensory and motor handicaps, and the relationship is a positive one. The component factor with the highest correlations is *physicalism*. Perhaps in coping with a sensory or motor handicap, a child can acquire a generalized set to analyze the problems of life in physical terms. The presence of strong fears in childhood also shows a slight tendency to relate—in this case negatively—to the components of *objectivism*.

The problems that suggest a tendency to act out aggressively—frequent fights and difficulties with teachers—tend to correlate positively with *environmental determinism* and negatively with *endogenism,* but they yield too little variance in the female subsample to correlate much with anything there. In any case, in combination with the contrasting correlations found for shyness, they seem to point to *endogenism vs. exogenism* as the second-order factor more closely related to social introversion-extraversion. The present correlations are all rather small, but that is hardly surprising when we consider the fact that the problem scores (each based on the presence or absence of a single checkmark) cannot be very reliable.

There were two other items in the biographical questionnaire that dealt with a problem area. In one item the subject was asked to indicate whether as a child, he or she was satisfied with his or her size and stature or regarded himself or herself as too short, too tall, too fat, or too thin. There was a similar item for the adolescent period. A score based on the number of dissatisfactions indicated for the two items failed to correlate significantly with any factor for the total sample. For women, it correlated positively with *quantitative orientation.*

In another item in the questionnaire subjects were asked to indicate the approximate age corresponding to the earliest life events they could recall. The reported age correlated negatively with *impersonal causality* for men and for the total sample and showed little relationship to anything else. I had suspected that subjectivists might dwell more on past personal experiences and remember earlier ones, but this expectation was not supported by the data. The meager findings are not surprising, however, for in other research I have found little relationship between early memories and personal-

ity variables in general.[1] Perhaps the content of the earliest
memories would prove more revealing, as Alfred Adler in particular
insisted, but this is something I have not attempted to study systematically.

Most of the remaining information about childhood provided by
the biographical questionnaire comes from an item in which subjects
were asked to indicate how much time (less than others, about as
much as others, or more than others their age) they had devoted in
childhood and adolescence to each of 10 activities. The activities included (1) active games or sports; (2) reading; (3) artwork; (4) making things (with paper, cloth, wood, metal, etc.); (5) collecting things
(stamps, rocks, shells, coins, dolls, etc.); (6) singing or playing a musical instrument; (7) talking to friends; (8) watching television or
listening to radio or records; (9) organized club activities; and (10)
dramatics. Each of these activities was scored separately, and the
correlations between these activities and the TOS factors for the
total sample are shown in Table 10.

Some of the activities yield nothing of significance. Perhaps the
clearest trend is that for active games and sports, which seems to be
an exogenist activity. It correlates positively with *environmental determinism* and negatively with *biological determinism* and *endogenism*. The activity that comes closest to displaying the opposite
pattern of associations is music. The same trends are clearly evident
in both sexes and are slightly more marked in women than men.
Once again, we have evidence that exogenism is associated in childhood with a disposition toward outward physically active expression.
There are no good correlates of *objectivism* here, though reading correlates negatively with two components—*factual orientation* and
physicalism. Within the female subsample, collecting, club activities,
and dramatics correlate positively either with *objectivism* or with its
component first-order factors.

There were two other items that pertained to club activities. In
these the subject was asked to indicate, for both high school and
college, the number of clubs to which he or she belonged and the
number of offices held. The sum of the numbers written for these
items provided an overall score for campus activity. This may represent a distinctive and meaningful kind of social behavior, but it fails
to yield any significant correlations with TOS factors.

ADULT EXPERIENCES

The biographical questionnaire contained items pertaining to
marital status, academic background in college, activities of a "self-

development" character, and preferences for various professional and recreational activities. Marital status showed little relationship to theoretical orientation, though in the female subsample *behavioral content emphasis* was associated with being currently married (*r* = .260).

Subjects were asked to indicate the extent to which they had been interested in each of 13 different academic areas when they were in college. The areas included English composition, literature, foreign languages, mathematics, social sciences, biological sciences, physical sciences, history, philosophy, art, music, drama, and physical education. Each area was rated on a five-point scale. The correlations between these interest scores and the TOS factors are shown in Table 11.

The area that most clearly correlates positively with *objectivism* and its components is physical sciences. Mathematics and biological sciences show similar patterns of correlations. The area that manifests the strongest negative relationship with *objectivism* and its components is music, and similar patterns are found for English composition and foreign languages. The correlations found for literature, social science, history, philosophy, art, and drama are negligible, at least for the total sample. On the basis of the correlations that are present, however, it appears that objectivists have a relatively strong interest in the natural sciences, while subjectivists have a relatively strong interest in the humanities (at least in language and music).

The area that relates most clearly to *endogenism vs. exogenism* is physical education. This correlates negatively with *biological determinism* and *endogenism* and positively with *environmental determinism*. Once again active physical expression goes with exogenism. There is no comparable pattern found for any other area, though mathematics has a significant positive correlation with *environmental determinism*. In the male subsample, music correlates negatively with *environmental determinism,* while in the female subsample, English composition correlates positively with *endogenism.*

Subjects were also asked whether they had ever majored in a field other than psychology. Approximately three-fourths of the subjects indicated that they had. The mere fact of having majored in something else probably has no particular meaning itself. (In men, it correlates positively with *biological determinism* and *endogenism,* while in women it correlates negatively with *quantitative orientation.*) Presumably the nature of the other major area provides another indicator of academic interests in college, though one may abandon a field because it has proved much less satisfying than one expected. The fields in which subjects had majored were coded in terms of the following eight categories: (1) language (including English, literature, foreign languages, speech, journalism); (2) social science and history (history, political science, sociology, economics); (3) natural science and mathematics (including the physical sciences, biological sciences, mathematics, engineering, premedical curriculum); (4) philosophy; (5) education; (6) fine arts (art, music, drama); (7) business (administration, secretarial studies, finance); and (8) other.

For purposes of analysis, the subjects who had majored in fields other than psychology (59 men and 59 women) were grouped in terms of their scores on the two second-order factors. Then, the objectivists (those scoring above average in factor I) were compared with the subjectivists (those scoring below average on factor I), and the endogenists (those scoring above average on factor II) were compared with the exogenists (those scoring below average on factor II) with respect to major areas.

The field that proved most relevant to the objectivism-subjectivism dichotomy was philosophy. All eight subjects who had majored in philosophy were subjectivists. This is consistent with the reasoning above if we view philosophy as one of the humanities. An interest in philosophy failed to correlate with factor I, however, and it is obvious that the field of philosophy houses both objectivists and subjectivists. Perhaps some of the eight former philosophy majors left that field because they found contemporary American philosophy a bit too "hardheaded" for their tastes. There is only one other significant trend for factor I—men who had majored in language tended to be objectivists. This trend is less pronounced than the one for philosophy, and for women we find an insignificant trend in the opposite direction (former language majors tending to be subjectivistic).

A significant effect for factor II is found for one area. Subjects who had majored in a social science or history tended to be endogenists. Again we have a significant effect for a domain wherein interest showed little correlation with theoretical orientation. It is tempting to apply the "dissatisfaction" rationale to all the significant effects here. Thus, subjectivists find philosophy too objectivistic, while objectivistic men find language and literature too subjectivistic, and endogenists find other social sciences and history too exogenist. Presumably psychology is sufficiently catholic to permit all these people to move in a direction that is more satisfying. We would need additional information to confirm such a rationale. Perhaps we should note, too, that these trends are less impressive than the sex difference apparent in nonpsychology majors. Most of these majors fall either into the language group or the natural science-mathematics group. It is quite apparent that female psychologists are much more likely to have had majors in the former group, while male psychologists are much more likely to have had majors in the latter group. There are obviously some sex-linked social pressures that affect the choice of a major and that are themselves quite independent of the student's "natural" intellectual orientation.

Undoubtedly the theoretical orientation of American psychologists is tempered to a great extent by the intellectual climate to which they have been exposed in American colleges and universities. It does not appear, however, that we can account very much for individual differences in orientation in terms of individual differences in areas of academic concentration. At the college level, individual differences in subject-matter concentration are probably more a consequence than a cause of the individual's basic intellectual orientation. To some extent, training in physics and chemistry may tend to produce objectivists, and certain courses in the humanities may tend to produce subjectivists, but I am suggesting that the converse effect is more pronounced—that students tend to concentrate in the physical sciences because their basic orientation is already objectivistic, and they tend to concentrate in the humanities because they are already inclined toward subjectivism.

Perhaps the same generalization could be applied to almost any adult experience that we might expect to have a molding influence on theoretical orientation. The one other type of adult experience covered by the biographical questionnaire was that of a therapeutic or growth-promoting kind. There were items dealing with four specific kinds of experiences—being in an encounter group, undergoing psychotherapy, practicing meditation, and keeping a personal journal or diary. For each of these the subject was asked to provide a rough indication of the amount of experience he or she had had. Undoubtedly each of these kinds of experience can affect a psychologist's intellectual outlook, but there is still better reason for expecting that a psychologist's intellectual outlook will determine whether he or she will seek out any of these experiences in search for greater self-understanding or personal growth. My data suggest essentially that subjectivists are more likely than objectivists to seek any or all of them.

All the significant correlations between these four kinds of experience and TOS factors are negative correlations with *objectivism* and its components. The encounter-groups variable correlates negatively with *behavioral content emphasis* for the total group. For some reason, it yields low correlations for women, but higher ones for the male supsample (wherein it correlates significantly with factors 3, 7, 8, and I). The experience of psychotherapy yields significant negative correlations with *impersonal causality, behavioral content emphasis, physicalism,* and *objectivism.* The practice of meditation yields significant correlations with *impersonal causality, behavioral content emphasis,* and *objectivism.* In contrast to encounter groups, it yields higher correlations for women than men (correlating with factors 1, 3, and I in the former group). The keeping of journals yields significant negative correlations with *factual orientation* and *behavioral content emphasis.* This is not too surprising in view of the fact that all four forms of experience require the individual to deal with his own subjective realm—his feelings, his images, his thought processes, his fantasies and dreams.

7. Interests, Values, Attitudes, and Cognitive Variables

INTEREST PATTERNS

The biographical questionnaire contained three items relating to the current interests of the subject. In the first item, the subject was asked to indicate degree of interest for each of 14 occupations. In the second, the subject was to indicate degree of interest for each of six professional activities within the field of psychology. In the third, the subject was to indicate degree of interest for each of 16 possible recreational activities. Each of the item elements was to be rated on a five-point scale.

The 14 occupations are indication in Table 12, which contains the correlations between those occupations and the TOS factors. The occupations were intended to cover a broad spectrum. They include fields (such as sales and business occupations) in which the average interest of psychologists is low, as well as fields (professional, scientific, and esthetic occupations) in which the average interest of psychologists is high. Many of these occupations correspond rather directly to the academic interest areas discussed in the preceding chapter. Thus, we might expect them to provide much the same information. So far as basic trends are concerned, this is certainly the case, but the correlations shown in Table 12 tend to be higher than the corresponding correlations in Table 11. Thus, *artist* yields higher correlations than *art, mathematician* yields higher correlations than *mathematics, novelist* yields higher correlations than *English composition* and *literature,* etc. Perhaps the most obvious reason is that the occupational item calls for present interests, while the academic interests that the subject had while in college reflect his orientation at an earlier point in life.

There are three occupations that are clearly correlated with *objectivism* and its components in a positive direction—engineer, mathematician, and physical scientist. The first of these represents the most concrete orientation, and it yields the highest pattern of correlations. Indeed it yields the highest positive correlation with every component of *objectivism* except *quantitative orientation,* where the highest correlation is for mathematician. The occupations that correlate negatively with *objectivism* and its components include artist, musician, novelist, and physician. Minister is clearly also a member of this cluster, but it yields significant correlations only for the male subsample, where it correlates negatively with *impersonal causality, behavioral content emphasis, elementarism, physicalism,* and *objectivism.* There is also a sex difference in the level of correlations for the artist and physician variables. The former correlates more substantially with *objectivism* and its components within the female subsample, while the latter yields higher correlations among men. Salesman and social worker also yield negative correlations with *objectivism* and its components, but none are significant.

Once again, we find that the objectivism-subjectivism polarity aligns with a division between the natural sciences and the arts or humanities. In a sense, engineering and medicine are both fields that involve applications of the natural sciences. In engineering, the focus is on the concrete world, and the application takes an impersonal, object-oriented form. In medicine, the focus is on people, and the application is designed to help them in some way. An interest in occupations concerned directly with people tends to go with subjectivism. On the other hand, none of the occupations shows much relationship to *endogenism* and its components. The one significant value obtained is a negative correlation for men between *environmental determinism* and musician.

The six professional activities to which the subject was asked to respond included teaching, research, writing, administrative work, counseling or psychotherapy, and serving as a consultant in the subject's own areas of expertise. The correlations between these activities and the TOS factors are shown in Table 13. For the total sample, research and counseling-psychotherapy yield the highest correlations. Research tends to correlate positively with *objectivism* and its components, while counseling-psychotherapy tends to correlate negatively. These patterns are more pronounced for the male subjects than for the female subjects. Another activity that relates negatively to components of *objectivism* is writing. In this case, the correlations are higher for women. Within the female subsample, writing has significant correlations with factors 1, 2, 3, and 7. The contrasting correlation profiles found for research and writing are interesting in view of the fact that these two activities commonly accompany each other in psychology. Indeed, the correlation between these two interests is .556, the highest for any pair of professional activities. Research, however, is a "natural" expression for the "objective," ordering, and scientific inclinations of the objectivist. An interest in writing, on the other hand, tends to entail more in the way of a need for theory or conceptualization, for as we turn from data gathering to writing, we move from observation to concepts. Thus, for both male and female subjects, it yields the highest (negative) correlations obtained with factor 1, *factual vs. theoretical orientation,* and it correlates more highly with that factor than with any other.

Endogenism vs. exogenism relates less clearly to professional activity interests. We found in the analysis of demographic data that extreme endogenists are more likely than exogenists to be engaged in research, but the present correlations show no relationship between this factor and research interests. There is a slight positive correlation between *environmental determinism* and an interest in consulting. For men, an interest in administration correlates positively with *biological determinism* and *endogenism,* while an interest in counseling or psychotherapy correlates negatively with these two TOS variables. For women and the combined sample, these correlations are all quite low.

The sixteen recreational activities listed in the biographical questionnaire included physically active recreation (hiking, swimming, active games), chess, card games, listening to music, dancing, conversing with friends, drawing pictures, watching sports events, watching a play or movie, attending a large party, visiting an art gallery, singing or playing a musical instrument, reading novels, reading poetry, reading science fiction, and reading nonfiction. The correlations between interest in these activities and TOS factors are shown in Table 14.

The clearest positive correlate of *objectivism* and its components is chess, the activity that most obviously stresses a kind of analytical thought—and an activity elected more often by mathematicians and engineers than by people in the arts. The correlations for chess tend to run higher in the male subsample, where a comparable pattern is also found for card games. The clearest negative correlates of *objectivism* and its components are the aesthetic production variables, drawing pictures and singing or playing a musical instrument. Dancing is clearly a part of this group so far as the female subsample is concerned. For some reason, its only significant correlation for men is a positive correlation with factor 1.

From the evidence on life-history variables, we might expect physically active recreation to relate negatively to *endogenism,* and it does, but not to a significant degree. Watching sports events does correlate negatively with *biological determinism* and *endogenism*. The best positive correlate of *endogenism* is watching a play or movie, which in the female subsample correlates positively with *biological determinism* and *endogenism* and negatively with *environmental determinism*. For women, reading science fiction shows a very similar pattern of correlations. Reading poetry does also, but to a lesser extent.

VALUES

It is difficult to draw a sharp line of division between interests and values. Whatever conceptual distinction we may make between the two terms, they represent characteristics that are bound to be closely associated. Thus, we might well expect correlations of TOS factors with value scales to yield much the same information as correlations with interest scales. The best-known instrument for assessing values is the Allport-Vernon-Lindzey Study of Values, which is often treated in vocational guidance work as an interest test.

One of the samples of respondents in the TOS research received a package consisting of the Study of Values, the Psycho-Epistemological Profile, and the General Beliefs questionnaire. These instruments were completed and returned by 62 men and 37 women, a total of 99 subjects. The Study of Values contains scales for assessing six basic value dimensions—theoretical, economic, aesthetic, social, political, and religious. The six variables correspond to six basic types of people distinguished by Eduard Spranger.

Sex differences are commonly found in all the Study of Values scales. In general, men score higher than women on the theoretical, economic, and political scales, while women score higher on the aesthetic, social, and religious scales. My sample shows a sex difference in the usual direction on every scale, but the sex differences are smaller than one finds in the general population and are overshadowed by a pattern that seems to be common to psychologists in general. My subjects, both men and women, tend to score higher than most people on the theoretical and aesthetic scales and lower on the economic and religious scales.

The correlations between the Study of Values scales and the TOS factors are shown in Table 15. It appears that the natural science–humanities polarity is represented in the former instrument by the theoretical and aesthetic scales. Theoretical value has the highest positive correlation with *objectivism,* and it correlates significantly with four of the component first-order factors. It correlates zero with factor 1. This is understandable when we consider the composition of the theoretical value scale. The subject who earns a high theoretical score is expressing a high regard for both the research and theoretical activities of scientists and for the rational and truth-seeking functions of the human mind in general. In short, a high score on the theoretical value scale is equally consistent with the factual-orientation and the theory-orientation poles of factor 1. The economic scale, which taps a practical, utilitarian outlook that tends to be pronounced in people in the business community and to some extent in engineers, also shows some positive correlation with *objectivism*. The remaining "masculine" scale, political value, also tends toward a positive relationship, but it manifests a significant correlation only for factor 2.

Aesthetic value shows the clearest alliance with subjectivism. It is interesting that its highest correlation is with factor 1. It clearly goes with a theoretical, as opposed to a factual, orientation. Of course, no activity of the scientist more closely resembles the process of artistic production than does the construction of theory. In many respects, a scientific theory is a work of art, and the criteria by which we judge it are quite analogous to those of aesthetic criticism. The social value scale, which focuses on a concern for human welfare, also correlates negatively with *objectivism*. The religious scale shows a faint tendency in the same direction, manifesting a significant correlation only with factor 2.

The Study of Values throws less light on *endogenism vs. exogenism*. The one value that yields significant correlations is aesthetic, which correlates negatively with *environmental determinism* and positively with *endogenism*. This is consistent with the life-history and interest data we have already considered, but it is too weak a pattern to warrant prolonged consideration.

One other instrument in my battery that is designed to measure values is the Survey of Interpersonal values (SIV) of Leonard V. Gordon. I had originally selected this test because I felt that theoretical orientation might be related to interpersonal needs and orientation. The SIV promised to provide some useful information about this realm without demanding much time on the part of subjects. It contains scales for six interpersonal values, which Gordon defines as follows:

> S—Support: Being treated with understanding, receiving encouragement from other people, being treated with kindness and consideration.
>
> C—Conformity: Doing what is socially correct, following regulations closely, doing what is accepted and proper, being a conformist.

R—Recognition: Being looked up to and admired, being considered important, attracting favorable notice, achieving recognition.

I—Independence: Having the right to do whatever one wants to do, being free to make one's own decisions, being able to do things in one's own way.

B—Benevolence: Doing things for other people, sharing with others, helping the unfortunate, being generous.

L—Leadership: Being in charge of other people, having authority over others, being in a position of leadership or power.[1]

When the scores for my sample are compared with the college-based norms provided by Gordon, it is apparent that my subjects tend to score a little above average on support, independence, and leadership, while they score extremely low on conformity. The correlations between the interpersonal values and the TOS factors are shown in Table 16.

The value that most clearly goes with objectivism is leadership. This correlates significantly in a positive direction with factor I and with four of its first-order components. For men, independence manifests approximately the same pattern of correlations. (For the female subsample, however, it has only nonsignificant *negative* correlations with all the objectivism factors.) The value that best corresponds to subjectivism is benevolence, which manifests significant negative correlations with factors 2, 4, and I. The correlation pattern for support tends weakly in the same direction. The SIV contains no good correlates of *endogenism* and its components.

Benevolence logically corresponds to the social value of the Study of Values, and Gordon's data indicate in fact that the highest correlation between the two instruments is the one for those two scales. Leadership logically corresponds to the political scale of the Study of Values, though it apparently has a slightly higher correlation with the theoretical scale of that test. The Leadership scale seems to express a personal need for power more directly than does any of the Allport-Vernon-Lindzey scales, though power is considered the essence of the political value. In any case, the SIV counterpart of objectivism-subjectivism is a polarity of leadership and benevolence. This seems basically to imply that in relationships with other people, the objectivist tends to value power and self-assertion, while the subjectivist considers it more important to respond to the needs of the other person. Insofar as the expression of power is indifferent to the needs and interests of the other person, we could say that the subjectivist tends to be person-oriented while the objectivist tends to be object-oriented. In making this distinction, I am not seeking to praise the one orientation and condemn the other. Person-orientation (e.g., as expressed in Buber's concept of the I-thou relationship) is strongly emphasized currently in the humanistic movement in psychology, but it is possible to see some value in both person-orientation and object-orientation. The latter can sometimes be quite socially beneficial—as in the work of a skilled surgeon, who must maintain some degree of detachment from the patient on the operating table.

THE *WELTANSCHAUUNG*

The questionnaire called General Beliefs is the product of an effort to capture some of the basic dimensions of the *Weltanschauung,* or the system of general attitudes, beliefs, and modes of perceiving that underlie an individual's basic orientation to the world.[2] It contains scales for six independent factors: (1) conventional theistic religion vs. nontheistic viewpoint, (2) future-productive vs. present-spontaneous orientation, (3) detachment vs. involvement, (4) relativism vs. absolutism, (5) scientism-determinism, and (6) optimism vs. pessimism. The correlations between these factors and the TOS factors are shown in Table 17.

The belief factor that yields the highest correlations with TOS factors is scientism-determinism, which is evidently the General Beliefs counterpart of objectivism. It correlates significantly with factors 2, 3, 4, 7, 8, and I. Its highest correlation is with *impersonal causality.* This is hardly surprising, because the subject who scores high on scientism-determinism essentially expresses a belief in the inherent lawfulness and predictability of all events, as well as a belief that for understanding and for solutions to our problems it is best to rely on science and scientific method. Like *objectivism,* scientism-determinism correlates positively with scientific and mechanical interests and negatively with social welfare interest.

Detachment also goes with objectivism. The detachment scale correlates significantly with TOS factors 3, 7, and I. This is consistent with the idea of scientific "objectivity" and with Linda Wyrick's evidence for the "personalization" variable in psychotherapy (which we considered in Chapter 5). Apparently the subjectivist is a little more likely than the objectivist to believe that it is important to be involved in the events that occur in his world, to make commitments, and to take the risk of getting hurt in the process. The objectivist tends to regard the maintenance of emotional distance as a wise policy.

There is apparently some tendency for both optimism and future-productive orientation (a value central to the Puritan ethic) to go with *objectivism,* but there is a barely significant correlation only for the latter. Relativism vs. absolutism tends to relate negatively to *objectivism* and its components, but only the correlation for *quantitative* orientation is significant. The relativism scale taps a dimension that affects judgments regarding truth, beauty, and moral virtue. In view of the score patterns found on college campuses, we might expect relativism to go with subjectivism, since the most relativistic scores have been found among fine arts students, while the most absolutistic have been found in engineering students. The present correlations for relativism are in the expected direction but weak.

Conventional theistic religion shows no relationship to the general factor of *objectivism,* but it correlates positively with *factual orientation* and negatively with *impersonal causality.* These correlations are consistent with those found for the religious scale of the Study of Values. A belief in personal will is often linked closely to theism in Christian theology. Hence the negative correlation with factor 2 is to be expected, but the reason for the correlation with *factual orientation* is not so obvious. Perhaps the speculative quality of theoretical orientation (the negative pole of factor 1) poses a threat to certain dogmatic beliefs.

Once again the correlates of *endogenism* prove less definitive than those of *objectivism.* Detachment appears to go with endogenism, correlating significantly with factors 5 and II. Perhaps this is an expression of an "introversive" quality that seems to be a part of the endogenist. In the endogenist, detachment could represent a way of withdrawing from threatening interaction with the environment. Scientism and optimism, on the other hand, show a slight tendency to go with exogenism, but none of the relevant correlations are significant.

COGNITIVE STYLE

There has been one attempt to relate the TOS factors to a dimension of cognitive style. In research for a doctoral dissertation, Marjorie Crago investigated the relationship between theoretical orientation and the dimension of complexity-simplicity.[3] A number of instruments have been used to assess complexity-simplicity, and these instruments often show little agreement with one another. Dr. Crago used four different measures of complexity—the Barron-Welsh Art Scale, Kelly's Role Construct Repertory Test (the REP test), Berkowitz's Complexity Preference Scale, and Budner's Intolerance of Ambiguity Scale. These four instruments and the TOS were administered to 50 psychologists, most of whom were faculty members or graduate students at the University of Arizona.

The Barron-Welsh Art Scale and the scales of Berkowitz and Budner were found to be moderately intercorrelated, but Kelly's REP test proved to be quite independent of these three. The Barron-Welsh, Berkowitz, and Budner scales can all be said to tap a tendency to prefer or an ability to tolerate complex stimuli as opposed to a tendency to reject or avoid them. In the REP test the subject performs a kind of sorting operation with the names of people that he knows. The names are presented in sets of three, and in each triad the subject is asked to indicate in what way two of the people named are similar to each other and different from the third. The complexity score in this test is based on the number of constructs that the subject invokes to account for the similarities and differences among his acquaintances. Thus, the REP test score reflects a tendency toward complexity in interpersonal perception, rather than a preference dimension. The high scorer distinguishes other people in terms of a great variety of qualities, while the low scorer tends to perceive and distinguish people in terms of a very limited set of categories or dichotomies.

The Barron-Welsh, Berkowitz, and Budner scales do not correlate significantly with any of the TOS factors. In fact, they yield only two correlations greater than .20. *Behavioral content emphasis* correlates −.222 with the Berkowitz scale and .212 with the Budner scale. The REP test, however, correlates fairly substantially with *objectivism* and its components. It correlates −.117 with factor 1, −.236 with factor 2, −.381 with factor 3, −.278 with factor 4, −.352 with factor 7, −.320 with factor 8, and −.402 with factor I. With a sample of 50 subjects, the correlations for factors 3, 7, 8, and I are significant. It appears that while *objectivism vs. subjectivism* may not be related to a general cognitive-style dimension of complexity-simplicity, it is related to complexity of interpersonal perception. Subjectivists tend to perceive and conceptualize people in a more complex way than do objectivists. The fact that the highest correlations for first-order factors are those for factors 3 and 7 suggests that the relative inclination toward simplicity of interpersonal perception on the part of the objectivist is linked to a tendency to avoid dealing with experiential variables and to think of people primarily in terms of fairly explicit behavioral variables.

WAYS OF KNOWING

Joseph Royce contends that there are four basic epistemologies, i.e., four basic ways of approaching reality or of knowing.[4] These include rationalism, intuitionism or metaphorism, empiricism, and authoritarianism. In seeking truth, we can rely on logical manipulation, on the immediate apprehension of symbolic meanings, on immediate sensory experience, or on the judgment of authority.

Royce says that different disciplines stress different epistemologies. Art stresses intuitionism. Philosophy and mathematics stress rationalism. Religion stresses a combination of intuitionism and rationalism, though in some religious sects there may be a heavier reliance on authoritarianism. Science generally stresses rationalism and empiricism, but there is also variation within science. The laboratory investigator may depend heavily on empiricism. The theorist may depend a bit more on rationalism and possibly intuitionism.

Royce has developed a questionnaire, the Psycho-Epistemological Profile (PEP), that is designed to assess relative dependence on three of these epistemologies. It contains scales for Metaphorism, Rationalism, and Empiricism. Research data are being gathered with the PEP on many different groups. In the TOS research, this instrument was part of the package that included the Study of Values and General Beliefs. Correlations between the PEP scales and the TOS factors are shown in Table 18.

Rationalism shows little relationship to the TOS factors. It does have barely significant positive correlations with factors 6 and 8. The latter is to be expected, since an interest in the mathematical realm should be accompanied by an inclination to rely on rational processes. It is a little more difficult to see why rationalism should relate particularly to *environmental determinism* or *exogenism*.

Metaphorism and empiricism, however, are clearly aligned respectively with subjectivism and objectivism. Metaphorism correlates negatively with *objectivism* and all its first-order components, while empiricism correlates positively with the same variables. Moreover, these correlations are all significant except that between *quantitative orientation* and metaphorism and that between *behavioral content emphasis* and empiricism.

The metaphorism scale contains items that express an interest in the arts, as well as items that stress the importance of imagination, feeling, emotional sensitivity, and concern for others. Thus, along with content pertaining rather directly to intuitive apprehension or a focus on symbolic meaning, it contains a variety of features that we have already found to be associated with subjectivism. With respect to the first-order components of factor I, this scale correlates most highly with factors 3 and 7. Thus, the individual who scores high on metaphorism is particularly inclined to stress the importance of experiential or subjective variables and to reject any effort to reduce the subjective to the objective. The concept of metaphorism, or intuitionism, itself implies a reliance on insights that do not depend heavily on immediate perception of specific external events.

The empiricism scale, as we would expect, contains items that stress accurate observation, realism, and "objectivity." Since the scientific method presumably embodies these features, we also find items pertaining to research, experimentation, and science in general. An interest in the natural sciences is conducive to the achievement of a high score, and we know from other data that this interest tends to accompany the objectivistic orientation. Royce's rationale, of course, suggests that an emphasis on immediate observation is the root element common to both the objectivistic orientation and the natural-science interest.

Royce has argued that we fall short in our understanding of the world to the extent that we rely on any of the basic epistemologies to the exclusion of others. In his terms, we are "encapsulated." There is a limit to what the human being is capable of knowing and understanding, but we can approach this limit if we freely utilize all the basic ways of knowing. The Western world on the whole has relied heavily on rationalism, though in recent times, with the increasing development and prominence of science, empiricism may have become the dominant epistemology. Royce joins Jung, Cassirer, Campbell, and others who stress the importance of symbols and myths, in contending that we need to be open to modes of understanding that we have neglected. He issues a plea for the development of the "unencapsulated man." This concept of the fully developed person essentially equates full development with manifold awareness. Royce deals with optimal development almost entirely in cognitive terms, but he regards his concept of the unencapsulated man as closely akin to Jung's idea of the fully individuated person. My own treatment of flexibility as a requisite of optimal functioning is parallel in many respects to Royce's concept of unencapsulation.[5]

The correlation between the TOS and PEP give us an idea of what pathways to understanding are emphasized by the people who adopt a particular theoretical perspective, but implicit in this association is the possibility that alternative pathways may be excluded. Both subjectivists and objectivists are capable of encapsulation. The objectivist may overrely on direct observation of external events. He may give little heed to his own feelings and fantasies, and he may be insensitive to symbolic meanings. The subjectivist is less likely to be guilty of this, but he may disparage the procedures of the objectivist. He may be a less accurate observer of external physical events, and he may have strong biases against the use of quantification and mathematical analysis. A symptom of encapsulation often found among people in the human potential movement is an inclination to view feelings as far more important than rational thought. There are many ways in which we can endeavor to make sense of ourselves and of the world around us. Can we afford to neglect any of them?

8. Personality

The TOS research battery contained four instruments that we have not yet considered. The package sent to one group of correspondents contained the Experience Inventory and the Myers-Briggs Type Indicator. These tests were completed and returned by 62 men and 44 women, or a total of 106 subjects. Another package contained the Sixteen Personality Factor Questionnaire (the 16PF) and the Personal Opinion Survey. These two tests were completed and returned by 51 men and 39 women, or a total of 90 subjects.

OPENNESS TO EXPERIENCE

The Experience Inventory is designed to assess openness to various kinds of experience.[1] A preliminary version of the instrument contained 114 items of highly varied content. The items were all designed to reflect openness, but the experiential content covered a wide assortment of associations, memories, ideas, impulses, feeling states, and fantasy and dream phenomena. The preliminary inventory was factor-analyzed, and the present inventory contains scales corresponding to seven large-variance factors found in that analysis. The scales are identified as follows:

1. Aesthetic sensitivity vs. insensitivity
2. Unusual perceptions and associations
3. Openness to theoretical or hypothetical ideas
4. Constructive utilization of fantasy and dreams
5. Openness to unconventional views of reality vs. adherence to mundane, material reality
6. Indulgence in fantasy vs. avoidance of fantasy
7. Deliberate and systematic thought

These scales are all scored in such a way that a high score represents greater openness to a given kind of experience. There is a weak general openness dimension (that could be extracted as a higher-order factor) common to these seven factors. Hence, the scales are moderately intercorrelated. The first six all tend toward positive intercorrelations. The seventh scale represents a mode of experience that tends to be negatively associated with that of the other scales.

The Experience Inventory deals with openness to various modes of perceiving, thinking, and feeling. One could argue that, despite the varied terrain covered by this instrument, it tends to favor a certain kind of inward-dwelling individual. In earlier research, the Experience Inventory (actually the preliminary version of it) and the Activity Checklist were both included in a complex battery that was analyzed. The Activity Checklist was designed to cover an openness expressed through varied action—it encompassed a wide range of social, recreational, and athletic activities. The checklist score generally correlated positively with the inventory factors, indicating that both instruments tapped some kind of general openness to experience. The correlations between the checklist variables and other battery variables, however, showed that it represented a very extraverted kind of openness, while the Experience Inventory factors did not. Whether we want to call the inward sensitivity tapped by the Experience Inventory an "introverted" openness depends on our definition of *introversion*. The inventory scores apparently have little to do with the kind of introversion measured by the Myers-Briggs Type Indicator. On the whole, they correlate most highly with the intuition-sensation polarity of that instrument (tending to be associated positively with intuition and negatively with sensation).

The correlations between the Experience Inventory factors and the TOS factors are shown in Table 19. I have argued before that fluid orientation, represented in the TOS by subjectivism, involves greater openness to the varied qualities of people and of human experience, and that the opposing, restrictive orientation sacrifices this openness for the sake of greater order and certainty. This position is supported in the present data by an overall pattern of negative correlations between inventory factors and *objectivism* and its components. The pattern of significant values, of course, is a bit more selective than this. There is a tendency for the substantial correlations to be concentrated in the third and fourth columns, and the inventory factors yield no significant correlations with TOS factors 1, 5, 6, and 8 or with *endogenism vs. exogenism*.

The sort of openness represented by the Experience Inventory, then, is particularly associated with experiential content emphasis and holism. To state the matter conversely, factors 3 and 4 *(behavioral vs. experiential content emphasis* and *elementarism vs. holism)* express at their low ends (or negative poles) a general openness to the varied content of human experience.

We should also note the variation among the rows of the table. Deliberate and systematic thought does not correlate significantly with any of the TOS factors, and indulgence in fantasy (which probably taps a certain motivational element in addition to openness) barely correlates significantly with just one factor (TOS factor 3). The inventory factor that yields the most substantial correlations is the factor of unconventional views of reality (vs. adherence to mundane, material reality). The subject who scores high on that variable is essentially an individual who is willing to entertain the idea of various kinds of events that defy simply material description or explanation—extrasensory perception, out-of-the-body travel, the presence on earth of extraterrestrial beings (as a reality behind some UFOs), etc. The unconventional-views variable manifests significant negative correlations not only with factor 3 *(behavioral content emphasis)* but also with factors 2 *(impersonal causality vs. personal will)* and 7 *(physicalism).* An insistence on generally understood material modes of explanation is likely to be particularly associated with high scores on factors 2 and 7. Factor 7 also has a significant (negative) correlation with aesthetic sensitivity. The explanation can no doubt be found in a literal-minded quality common to the entities that I have called physicalism and esthetic insensitivity. The subject who scores low on the first Experience Inventory factor leans toward the view that all art should be representative and that good poems should be fully translatable into rationally understandable prose.

THE EXPERIENCE OF CONTROL

The Personal Opinion Survey (POS) is also a factored instrument.[2] It is designed to measure several basic dimensions of the experience of control. It contains scales for the following seven factors:

1. Achievement through conscientious effort
2. Personal confidence in ability to achieve mastery
3. Capacity of humanity to control its destiny vs. supernatural power or fate
4. Successful planning and organization
5. Self-control over internal processes
6. Control over large-scale social and political events
7. Control in immediate social interaction

The correlations among these factors are generally very low; there does not appear to be any sort of general control factor common to the entire set. The POS contains a mixture of first-person and third-person items. Some of the scales (specifically 2, 4, 5, and 7) are concerned with the personal experience of the subject. Scales 1 and 3 are concerned primarily with the capacity of people in general for exerting some kind of control, while scale 6 contains both first-person and third-person items.

The correlations between the POS factors and the TOS factors are shown in Table 20. The significant correlations are confined to the first three POS factors. POS factors 2 and 3 both correlate significantly in a positive direction with *objectivism* and with several of its component first-order factors. POS factor 2 correlates with TOS factors 3, 4, and 8, while POS factor 3 correlates with TOS factors 2, 3, 7, and 8. In the one case, belief in the subject's own capacity for control goes with objectivism, while in the other, a belief in the capacity of humanity goes with objectivism.

To account for these relationships, we may note that objectivism itself entails a need for control. Presumably the objectivist is more intent than the subjectivist on dealing with events in a way that insures control, predictability, and certainty. It does not necessarily follow from this that he will actually achieve greater control, but the objectivist does tend to confine his efforts to areas of observation where a high degree of control is possible. Within the more limited realm to which he attends in his scientific pursuits, he should achieve and experience more control than the subjectivist. The correlation with POS factor 2 suggests that this experience is characteristic not only of the theoretical territory to which he addresses his work but of his personal life as well—though not the whole of his personal life. We should note that there are other POS factors that deal with personal control. POS factor 5 is concerned with control over one's thoughts, feelings, and bodily processes, and POS factor 7 is concerned with one's ability to influence other people in immediate interaction. POS factor 2, in contrast, has more to do with such realms as athletic and intellectual achievement, particularly the latter. It thus has more to do with what an intellectual individual is able to accomplish in his work. The implication of the relationship between objectivism and POS factor 2, then, is that the objectivist not only has a greater need to experience control over the focal content of his intellectual endeavors, but also tends to succeed in achieving and experiencing more of this control. The kinds of personal control expressed by POS factors 5 and 7, on the other hand, show little relationship to theoretical orientation.

POS factor 3 is not concerned with the control experienced by the subject himself. The individual who scores high on that factor contends essentially that humanity is capable of building a just society, acting to eliminate war, and controlling its own evolution and various natural physical phenomena. At least some of the items imply a human capacity that depends on the accumulation of scientific information and on the use of scientific methods. Thus, a high score expresses in part a faith in the power of science. As we already know from other evidence, such an outlook tends to accompany objectivism.

The POS throws a fresh light on the other second-order factor. POS factors 1 and 2 both correlate negatively with *endogenism*. In both cases, there is a still higher positive correlation with *environmental determinism* and a nonsignificant negative correlation with *biological determinism*. Thus, the individual who stresses environmental influence, the exogenist, tends to believe that people generally can accomplish many things if they try hard enough and to believe also that he himself has the capacity required for accomplishment in various realms—mathematical, mechanical, scientific, athletic, and linguistic. The idea common to both of the POS variables is the possibility of setting a goal and achieving it as a result of appropriate effort. Why should the exogenist be more inclined than the endogenist to accept this idea? Both biological determinism and environmental determinism imply the possibility of our being controlled by forces or events over which we have no control and of which we may even be unaware. The biological determinist stresses determinants built into the organism, while the environmental determinist stresses the learning process. The latter position, however, implies greater modifiability, greater possibility of departure from the form dictated by the original mold. Thus, the environmentalist may contend that a demonic psychologist can take any normal infant (or any "dozen healthy infants") and turn him, by proper arrangement of environmental contingencies, into a beggar, thief, artist, or saint. Implicit in such a view, of course, is the further possibility that the infant will become a psychologist himself and acquire the information that will enable him to arrange his own contingencies. Indeed, he may learn to lead a very successful and admirable life without even studying psychology.

In emphasizing the influence of the social environment, as against a comparatively rigid biological destiny, and in stressing learning over maturational change, the exogenist accords great power to the environment. He knows, however, that environments can be changed. Perhaps the individual can change his own environment or elect a different one. It is clearly possible to reconcile the idea of self-control with the exogenist position, and there is undoubtedly much variation in views on this among people who score in the exogenist direction. As we know from earlier chapters, both "Skinnerians" and "Rogerians" lean toward exogenism. I think, however, that the key to the association between exogenism and POS factors 1 and 2 lies in the idea of modifiability, or the possibility of change in many directions, and not in any concept of personal will (since the latter is represented by the negative pole of TOS factor 2, which is definitely not a part of the pattern under consideration).

JUNGIAN TYPAL DIMENSIONS

The Jungian personality typology has a special relevance for any inquiry of the present sort. It represents one of the most elaborate theoretical efforts to capture in a typological scheme the basic modes of variation in our experience of the world. According to Jung, these are the basic modes that underlie individual differences in intellectual production and intellectual orientation. Thus, in discussing introversion and extraversion, Jung contends that these two fundamental attitudes are the source of two differing streams in Western philosophy that can be traced to Plato and Aristotle respectively. The logic is not limited to philosophy, of course, for no major personality theorist has pursued more diligently than Jung the thesis that every theory—and most certainly every psychological theory—bears the personal imprint of its creator.

Jung's typology is essentially a three-dimensional system. It assumes an attitude polarity of extraversion and introversion and two psychic-function polarities. One of the latter polarities is that of thinking and feeling, and the other is that of sensation and intuition. Thinking and feeling are considered rational functions— functions concerned with the formation of a judgment. Thinking is directed toward truth judgments, while feeling is directed toward value judgments. Sensation and intuition are considered irrational functions, because they are concerned not with judgment but with perception, with the process whereby content comes into awareness. One of these functions depends more directly on immediate sensory content, while the other depends heavily on unconscious processes and is directed less to what is immediately present than to possibilities and symbolic meanings implicit in what is present.

The typal system assumes that the two components of each of these polarities tend to be somewhat incompatible—though a reconciliation can be achieved—and that every individual tends to favor one of the components in conscious functioning and to suppress its opposite (which continues to operate on an unconscious level). In the course of development, the consciously dominant attitude is usually first apparent. Then one of the four functions emerges as the *superior* function, with its opposite being accorded least conscious development and hence being the *inferior* function. Still later a balance may be evident with respect to the remaining pair of functions, and the one that is favored there will tend to serve as a function auxiliary to the superior function.

The Jungian dimensions have never been captured in a fully satisfactory way in any psychometric instrument because the variables on which Jung is actually focusing are manifested rather indirectly in behavior and often elude self-awareness. Thus, the numerous scales that have been constructed to measure introversion-extraversion tend in the main to center on what might be called social introversion vs. social extraversion—whether the individual tends to be shy, aloof, relatively inaccessible, private, etc., or whether he is outgoing, sociable, freely expressive, at ease in large groups, etc. This is not quite the Jungian dimension, but only a moderately reliable expression of it. Jung is dealing with what he calls attitudes, not behavior traits. For Jung, the extravert is one whose interest and attention are centered on the objective realm (the realm of people and "objects" outside, in the environment) and whose actions and decision tend to be governed rather directly by objective events and circumstances. The introvert is one whose interest and attention are centered on the subjective realm (the realm of his own psychological processes) and whose actions and decisions tend to be governed more by subjective considerations (so that response to the stimuli and demands of the environment tends to be less direct and immediate). An extravert in the Jungian sense will tend to be more gregarious than his introverted counterpart, but this is not inevitable. There are shy engineers and socially active spiritual leaders who clearly defy any simple rule about an alignment between the Jungian concepts and the dimension that is more often assessed by questionnaires. Obviously when we gather data with any instrument designed to measure Jungian dimensions, we must attempt to understand what is actually being measured before we draw any conclusions from our data.

The best-known instrument designed to assess the typal dimensions is the Myers-Briggs Type Indicator. In the TOS research this test was included in the same package as the Experience Inventory. Two subjects who completed the Experience Inventory failed to complete the Type Indicator. Hence I obtained responses from 104 subjects (43 women and 61 men). The Type Indicator yields scores for eight variables—extraversion (E), introversion (I), sensation (S), intuition (N), thinking (T), feeling (F), judgment (J), and perception (P). The eight scores are somewhat redundant, since the scores for E and I are based largely, though not entirely, on the same set of items (oppositely keyed). The same is true for S and N, for T and F, and for J and P. The use of separate scores for the two components of each polarity is apparently intended to facilitate the assignment of subjects to types. For purposes of statistical treatment, however, the eight scores are reduced to four indexes: EI, SN, TF, and JP. Each of these indexes is derived in such a way that the second letter of the combination represents the high end of the scale. Thus, the high ends of the four scales are introversion, intuition, feeling, and perception respectively.

Each of the four indexes is also scored in such a way that a score of 100 is assumed to represent a point of division between contrasting types. It may be of interest to note that the mean scores for the male subjects in my sample (for EI, SN, TF, and JP respectively) are 93.59, 119.95, 101.10, and 97.59. The means for the female subjects are 104.16, 127.19, 107.37, and 103.67. Those for the total sample are 97.96, 122.94, 103.69, and 99.69. The most marked trend here is for scores in the direction of intuition. According to the test manual, the Strong Vocational Interest Blank scale that correlates most highly with SN is *psychologist*. Thus, an interest pattern that is characteristic of psychologists tends to be associated with a high SN score. It is not surprising, then, the psychologists as such score high on the scale. Both the men and the women also score somewhat in the feeling direction. On EI, the men tend to score in the extraversive direction, while the women score in the introversive direction. On the JP scale, the men tend toward judgment, while the women tend toward perception.

Essentially the same information can also be stated in terms of the frequencies found for each typal disposition. Thus, on the EI index, 40 men (out of 61) and 18 women (out of 43) score in the extraverted direction, as opposed to 21 and 25, respectively, scoring in the introverted direction. On the SN index, 12 men and 5 women score on the sensation side, as opposed to 49 and 38 on the intuition side. On the TF index, 29 men and 15 women score on the thinking side, with 32 and 28 on the feeling side. On the JP index, 34 men and 20 women score on the judgment side, with 27 and 23 on the perception side. In terms of the Myers-Briggs type notation, the modal type for the men is ENFJ, while that for the women is INFP, and that for the total sample is ENFJ. The JP index is assumed to indicate whether the function on which the individual relies most heavily is a rational (judgmental) function or an irrational (perceptual) function. Hence, in the four-letter type notation, the last letter would indicate which of the other letters denotes the superior function. If we translate the Myers-Briggs notion into Jungian terms, the modal male in the sample is a feeling extravert whose auxiliary function is intuition, and the modal female is an intuitive introvert whose auxiliary function is feeling.

The correlations between the four indexes and the TOS factors are shown in Table 21. I have shown the correlations for the male and female subsamples separately, in part because there are some minor sex differences in the correlations, but also because the T and F variables are scored somewhat differently for men and women. Hence the combination of male and female data for TF is not entirely legitimate.

The first Myers-Briggs variable, EI, relates most clearly to factors 5, 6, and II. For males, for females, and for the total group, it correlates positively with *biological determinism* and *endogenism* and negatively with *environmental determinism.* For the total group, all three correlations are significant, while two are significant for each of the subgroups. Here we have the most definite evidence up to this point that endogenists tend to be introverted, while exogenists tend to be extraverted. In interpreting this finding, we should probably note that EI is essentially concerned with social introversion vs. social extroversion if we are to judge from item content. In effect, the individual who scores high describes himself as quiet and reserved, while the individual who scores low describes himself as gregarious, talkative, and socially expressive. This is consistent with the correlations found between the Type Indicator and the scales of the Strong Vocational Interest Blank (SVIB).[3] EI tends to manifest its highest positive correlations with the scales for technical-scientific occupations and its highest negative correlations with the scales for "social uplift" and business contact occupations.

It should be noted that the present data provide independent confirmation of an association between *endogenism vs. exogenism* and social introversion-extraversion, since the life-history data that pointed in this direction were obtained from a different sample of subjects. Recognizing that there is some relationship between social introversion-extraversion and the Jungian dimension, can we properly infer that endogenism really goes with introversion in the Jungian sense (an investment of psychic energy or interest in the subjective realm)? It happens that such an association is quite consistent with Jung's own reasoning. In *Psychological Types,* Jung compares his own theoretical outlook with those of Freud and Adler.[4] He contends that the Freudian position is extraverted, while those of Adler and himself are introverted. The implication is that Freud was an extravert, while Adler and Jung were introverts. From what we know of the lives of Freud and Adler, this is at best an oversimplification of the facts, but it can be argued that during the periods of theoretical production on which Jung's argument rests, Freud was struggling against his own basic introversion and attempting to function as an extravert, while the more basic extraversion later evident in Adler (both in his personality and in his theorizing) had not yet emerged.[5] In any case, Jung's analysis of the theoretical systems of Freud and Adler focuses primarily on the weight that they attach to various possible determinants of character. The Freudian position is said to be extraverted because Freud emphasizes the molding influence of the social environment. This is particularly true of Freud's work prior to 1900 and somewhat less so after the formulation of the theory of psychosexual development. The Adlerian position is held to be introverted because it attaches greater importance to subjective determinants, such as the will to power and guiding fictions. Jungian theory also emphasizes the roles of determinants that arise in the inner world, particularly those from the collective unconscious.

By focusing on alleged determinants of personality or behavior, Jung is arguing in effect that the exogenist position is extraverted, while the endogenist position is introverted. If we apply this idea to Freud, Adler, and Jung, we may be able to build a better case for it than Jung himself did if we take developmental progressions in these theorists into account. Jung wrote *Psychological Types* rather early and was not in a good position at the time to do this. If we take the whole of Freud's work into account, we might consider him more endogenist than Adler. Certainly, he stands higher on *biological determinism*. His early writings reflect a sort of Lockean environmentalism, however, and the biological emphasis comes after 1900. An emphasis on subjective determinants appears early in Adler's work, but his writings show progressively increasing attention to social interaction. In his later work, he emphasizes the family context as a source of personality traits, and he sees *Gemeinschaftsgefühl* (a feeling of relatedness to other individuals and to humanity) as the most central quality of a fully developed person. The changes in Adler's writings parallel a shift in his own pattern of living, from that of a very aloof bookworm (whom Ernest Jones characterizes as "morose and cantankerous"[6]) to that of a warm, outgoing man who liked to be surrounded almost constantly by people. Jung's *Psychological Types* marks the beginning of a period of half a lifetime in which Jung was to probe more and more deeply into the inner world. It also marks the end of a period of inner struggle in Jung himself, a period (perhaps essentially from 1914 to 1919) from which he emerged with a more consistently introverted outlook and lifestyle.

The Myers-Briggs variable that relates most clearly to *objectivism vs. subjectivism* is TF. TF has a significant negative correlation with factor I for men, for women, and for the total sample. Its correlations with factors 1 and 4 are rather weak, but it has significant negative correlations with factors 2 and 3 for men and with factors 2, 3, 7, and 8 for the total sample. The first-order factor that correlates best with TF is *behavioral vs. experiential content emphasis*. Thus, an emphasis on feeling tends to go with subjectivism and its constitutents (particularly, behavioral content emphasis). In terms of Jungian theory, the thinking type is truth-oriented and may seek truth either in the outer realm of concrete facts (if extraverted) or in the inner realm of ideas (if introverted). The feeling type is concerned more with value judgments, with deciding whether things are good or bad, beautiful or ugly, desirable or undesirable. The feeling extravert tends to find positive value in the outer realm and his judgments tend to be greatly influenced by the people he encounters and by tradition. The feeling introvert is more likely to find positive value in his own subjective world and to view the outer condition in negative terms. This does not seem to be quite the dimension reflected in the Type Indicator items. The responses scored for thinking stress logic, consistency, impartiality, deliberateness, and firmness, while those scored for feeling refer to such qualities as compassion, sentiment, devotion, and gentleness. My overall impression of the scale is that the truth element is underemphasized on the thinking side (though the stress on logic is consistent with Jungian theory), while the feeling responses emphasize the extraverted expression of the feeling type. Nevertheless, the TF scale probably corresponds roughly to the Jungian dimension.

Perhaps the correlations with the Study of Values, which are cited in the Myers-Briggs test manual, illustrate the partial correspondence I see here. TF has its highest positive correlation with social value and its highest negative correlation with theoretical value, while its correlation with aesthetic value is essentially zero. The correlations with theoretical and social are probably consistent with Jungian theory, but a straightforward measure of feeling (rather than just extraverted feeling) would probably have as high a positive correlation with aesthetic value as with social value.

The alignment of the objectivism-subjectivism dimension with the thinking-feeling dimension of Jungian theory—even if we choose to quibble with the present measurement of the latter—still makes good sense. Subjectivists tend to show a greater concern with values and with the expression of them in commitment and involvement than do objectivists, and they deal in theory with a wider range of human experiences, such as love, that involve what Jung would call feeling. Objectivists are more likely to avoid this subject matter, and their approach to theory and research entails a stronger adherence to a tradition that stresses scientific "detachment" and a value-free quest for truth. The correlations we noted earlier between TOS factors and interests and between TOS factors and General Beliefs factors are consistent with this picture.

The SN scale also shows some relationship (negative) to *objectivism vs. subjectivism,* but there the significant correlations are confined to factors 1 and 3 for the total sample and to factor 1 for men. At least for men, however, intuition clearly goes with theoretical (as opposed to factual) orientation, while sensation goes with factual orientation. We might have expected a stronger pattern than this, since the Psycho-Epistemological Profile also contains two variables (metaphorism and empiricism) that correspond to intuition and sensation, and these correlated substantially with *objectivism vs. subjectivism* and its components.

According to Jungian theory, the perceptions of the sensation type emphasize the immediate data of sensory experience. These data tend to be construed by extraverts in terms of outer things and events (the external stimuli) and by introverts in terms of the sensations per se. The intuition type rapidly moves from the immediate data to meanings and possibilities. The Type Indicator responses scored for sensation stress fact, realism, common sense, and conventionality. Those scored for intuition stress theory, abstraction, imagination, and unconventionality. The scale content corresponds in part to the Jungian dimension, but the Jungian focus on symbolic meaning seems to be largely replaced by an emphasis on abstraction. In view of the scale's emphasis on the factual and concrete as opposed to the theoretical and abstract, it is hardly surprising that SN correlates best with TOS factor 1. From the standpoint of Jungian theory, however, this dichotomy is not so much a matter of sensation vs. intuition as it is extraverted thinking vs. introverted thinking.

The remaining significant findings for the Myers-Briggs Type Indicator are confined to the female subsample. In that group, TF correlates with *endogenism* and its components. Whatever the reason for this, it is balanced by an insignificant trend in the opposite direction for men, and this washes out the effect altogether for the total sample. For women, the JP variable also correlates negatively with factors 4, 8, and I. Thus, an emphasis on judgment (rational functions) goes with an emphasis on details and on the use of quantitative methods and description, while an emphasis on perception (irrational functions) goes with an emphasis on qualities and wholes. In terms of item content, judgment responses emphasize planning, organization, and deliberateness, while perception responses emphasize spontaneity, impulsiveness, and resistance to planning and order. The correlation pattern makes sense, but it is not clear why it is confined to the female subjects.

GENERAL PERSONALITY FACTORS

Probably no researcher has devoted greater effort to defining the major dimensions of personality through factor-analytic research than Raymond B. Cattell. One of the most widely used factored personality inventories is the Sixteen Personality Factor Questionnaire (the 16 PF), which was produced in Cattell's laboratory. This instrument yields scores for the following 16 factors. In identifying these, I present the letter symbols and technical labels that have been used widely in the literature on the 16PF and related instruments, as well as the popular description suggested on the test profile sheet. The popular description (presented in parentheses) will convey the meaning of each factor somewhat better to the reader unfamiliar with the instrument. I might note also that in the case of each bipolar factor description, the first part corresponds to the high end of the scale:

1. Factor A: Affectothymia (outgoing, warmhearted, easy-going, participating) vs. sizothymia (reserved, detached, critical, cool)
2. B: Intelligence
3. C: Higher ego strength (emotionally stable, faces reality, calm) vs. lower ego strength (affected by feelings, emotionally less stable, easily upset)
4. E: Dominance (assertive, independent, aggressive, stubborn) vs. submissiveness (humble, mild, obedient, conforming)
5. F: Surgency (happy-go-lucky, heedless, gay, enthusiastic) vs. desurgency (sober, prudent, serious, taciturn)
6. G: Stronger superego strength (conscientious, perse-

vering, staid, rule-bound) vs, weaker superego strength
(expedient, a law to himself, bypasses obligations)

7. H: Parmia (venturesome, socially bold, uninhibited,
spontaneous) vs threctia (shy, restrained, diffident, timid)

8. I: Premsia (tender-minded, dependent, overprotected,
sensitive) vs. harria (tough-minded, self-reliant, realistic,
no-nonsense)

9. L: Protension (suspicious, self-opinionated, hard to
fool) vs. alaxia (trusting, adaptable, free of jealousy, easy
to get on with)

10. M: Autia (imaginative, wrapped up in inner urgencies,
careless of practical matters, bohemian) vs. praxernia
(practical, careful, conventional, regulated by external re-
alities, proper)

11. N: Shrewdness (shrewd, calculating, worldly, penetrat-
ing) vs. artlessness (forthright, natural, artless, sentimen-
tal)

12. O: Guilt proneness (apprehensive, worrying, depres-
sive, troubled) vs. untroubled adequacy (placid, self-
assured, confident, serene)

13. Ql: Radicalism (experimenting, critical, liberal, analytical, free-thinking) vs. conservatism (conservative, respect-
ing established ideas, tolerant of traditional difficulties)

14. Q2: Self-sufficiency (self-sufficient, prefers own decisions, resourceful) vs. group adherence (group-dependent,
a "joiner" and sound follower)

15. Q3: High self-concept control (controlled, socially precise, self-disciplined, compulsive) vs. low integration
(casual, careless of protocol, untidy, follows own urges)

16. Q4: High ergic tension (tense, driven, overwrought,
fretful) vs. low ergic tension (relaxed, tranquil, torpid, un-
frustrated)

It is possible to derive several higher-order factors from these
16. The two that are best established are an anxiety factor and a
factor of introversion vs. extraversion. The anxiety factors loads factors L, O, and Q4 positively and factors C, H, and Q3 negatively.
The introversion factor loads factors Q1 and Q2 positively and A, F,
and H negatively. I included Form A of the 16PF in the package
that contained the Personal Opinion Survey, and I received completed forms from 90 subjects (51 men and 39 women). The correlations between the 16PF scales and the TOS factors are shown in
Table 22.

The 16PF variables that show the clearest relationship to *objectivism vs. subjectivism* are A, I, M, and Q1. Of these, the best correlate is I (Premsia), which has significant negative correlations with TOS factors 2, 3, 7, and I. The correlations of premsia with *objectivism* and its components tend to run a little higher still in the male subsample but are all weak and nonsignificant for women. The next best correlate is Q1 (radicalism), which has significant positive correlations with factors 2, 3, 7, 8, and I. These correlations are also higher in men than in women. Variable A (affectothymia) is another variable that tends to relate negatively with *objectivism,* but the only significant correlation for the total sample is with factor 8. This correlation is relatively high for both subgroups, but there is a more substantial pattern of negative correlations for the female subgroup, which yields significant values for factors 3, 7, and I. Variable M (autia) shows a more curious pattern. In the male subsample, it shows significant positive correlations with factors 2, 3, 7, and I, and the remaining nonsignificant correlations are positive. The pattern is almost totally reversed for the female group, where we find significant negative correlations with factors 1 and 4. Apart from the values for A, I, M, and Q1, there are just a few scattered significant values for *objectivism* and its components. For men and for the total sample, C correlates negatively with factor 8, while Q4 correlates negatively with factor 1. For women, F correlates negatively with factor 4, while G correlates positively with factor 1.

Overall, the 16PF variables that show the most consistent patterns are A, I, and Q1. Radicalism (Q1) is a positive correlate of *objectivism.* This makes sense, inasmuch as the responses of a subject who scores high on Q1 reflect a rather critical, analytical, experimental outlook that goes with the natural science tradition. Premsia (I) is the best negative correlate. At the high end, it is characterized by a kind of emotional sensitivity that Cattell regards as a product of a protective family environment in childhood. Variables Q1 and I respectively are probably the best representatives within the 16PF of the thinking and feeling functions—and also of the theoretical and aesthetic values. Affectothymia (A) is also a negative correlate of *objectivism.* Like premsia, it could be said to represent a kind of emotional sensitivity, but a kind expressed in a more social form—as empathy and concern. High scores on A probably bear some relationship to social value, and on this account we might expect them to go with subjectivism.

From the evidence found for other instruments, we might expect *endogenism* and its components, *biological determinism* and *environmental determinism,* to correlate best with the components of the second-order questionnaire factor of introversion vs. extraversion. None of the pertinent 16PF variables correlates significantly with factors 5, 6, and II, however, and Q2 is the only one that shows much of a trend in the appropriate direction. This variable (Q2) does correlate positively with factors 5 and II and negatively with factor 6, with correlations of approximately the same magnitude appearing for both sexes. Thus, there is at least a suggestion that endogenists tend to be relatively self-sufficient and exogenists more group-dependent.

The only 16PF variable that yields a significant value for factor 5, 6, or II is variable I (premsia vs. harria), which correlates negatively with factor 6 and just fails to yield a significant positive correlation with II. These correlations run a bit higher in men and lower in the female subgroup. This points to an emotional sensitivity that would be characteristic of endogenists and not of exogenists. In view of Cattell's contention that this sensitivity is a consequence of a protective family environment, this evidence seems consistent with the life-history data we have examined.

For other 16PF variables there is no consistent pattern across sexes. Thus, variable O has a significant negative correlation with factor 5 for men, but there is a small positive correlation for women. For women, Q3 correlates .408 with factor 6, but for men the correlation is close to zero. With respect to the entire pattern of correlations between 16PF variables and TOS factors, there are many curious sex differences. Perhaps there are important sex differences in the life experiences and selection of psychologists that should be examined in future research in this area.

9. An Overview of Psychological Patterns

Psychological theory is the work of many hands. It is, in many ways, a curious sort of crazy quilt, for its creators are a very heterogeneous crew. The limited material available on the lives of psychologists gives us some impression of the range of personalities who have attained prominence in this field. Consider the following fragments from the autobiographical accounts given by four major theorists of their early years:

> 1. My disunion with myself and uncertainty in the world at large led me to an action which at the time was quite incomprehensible to me. I had in those days, a yellow, varnished pencil case of the kind commonly used by primary-school pupils, with a little lock and the customary ruler. At the end of this ruler I now carved a little manikin, about two inches long, with frock coat, top hat, and shiny black boots. I colored him black with ink, sawed him off the ruler, and put him in the pencil case, where I made him a little bed. I even made a coat for him out of a bit of wool. In the case I also placed a smooth, oblong blackish stone from the Rhine, which I had painted with water colors to look as though it were divided into an upper and lower half, and had long carried around in my trouser pocket. This was *his* stone. All this was a great secret. Secretly I took the case to the forbidden attic at the top of the house (forbidden because the floorboards were worm-eaten and rotten) and hid it with great satisfaction on one of the beams under the roof—for no one must ever see it! I knew that not a soul would ever find it there. No one could discover my secret and destroy it. I felt safe, and the tormenting sense of being at odds with myself was gone. In all difficult situations, whenever I had done something wrong or my feelings had been hurt, or when my father's irritability or my mother's invalidism oppressed me, I thought of my carefully bedded-down and wrapped-up manikin and his smooth, prettily colored stone. From time to time— often at intervals of weeks—I secretly stole up to the attic

when I could be certain that no one would see me. Then I clambered up on the beam, opened the case, and looked at my manikin and his stone. Each time I did this I placed in the case a little scroll of paper on which I had previously written something during school hours in a secret language of my own invention.[1]

2. In 1890, when I was 12 years of age my family moved to Greenville, South Carolina, a village of 20,000 souls where I entered the public schools, passing through grammar school and high school. I have few pleasant memories of those years. I was lazy, somewhat insubordinate, and, so far as I know, I never made about a passing grade. I used to have a friend by the name of Joe Leech with whom I boxed every time my teacher left the room, boxed until one or the other drew blood. "Nigger" fighting was one of our favorite going-home activities. Twice I was arrested, once for "nigger" fighting, and the second time for shooting off firearms inside the city limits.[2]

3. I was a dreamy youngster all through these grammar school years, so lost in fantasy most of the time that my absent-mindedness was legendary. I was teased a great deal about this and called "Professor Moony," an absent-minded comic strip character of the period. I was buried in books—stories of Indian and frontier life to the extent that I could lay hands on them, but *anything* was grist to my mill. If there was nothing else, I read the encyclopedia or even the dictionary."[3]

4. I was always building things. I built roller-skate scooters, steerable wagons, sleds, and rafts to be poled about on shallow ponds. I made seesaws, merry-go-rounds, and slides. I made slingshots, bows and arrows, blow guns and water pistols from lengths of bamboo, and from a discarded water boiler a steam cannon with which I could shoot plugs of potato and carrot over the houses of our neighbors. I made tops, diabolos, model airplanes driven by twisted rubber bands, box kites, and tin propellers which could be sent high into the air with a spool-and-string spinner. I tried again and again to make a glider in which I myself might fly.

I invented things, some of them in the spirit of the outrageous contraptions which Rube Goldberg was publishing in the *Philadelphia Inquirer* (to which, as a good Republican, my father subscribed). For example, a friend and I used to gather elderberries and sell them from door to door, and I built a flotation system which separated ripe from green berries. I worked for years on the design of a perpetual motion machine. (It did not work.)[4]

None of these fragments is sufficient to provide a picture of a total person, but they are probably sufficient to suggest that the lives into which we are glimpsing belong to four distinctly different people. As we examine these lives in further detail and depth, we find many features that seem to have a direct bearing on the theoretical positions ultimately adopted by the four people. At present, a comprehensive understanding of the relationship between personal characteristics and intellectual orientation is a bit beyond our grasp, and we may need to explore this relationship by a variety of routes. The analysis of autobiographic material holds much promise for the psychology of psychology. In the work I have reported in this book, however, I have employed a somewhat different strategy in an effort to obtain a broadscale view, and I should like to summarize the salient features of my findings.

I endeavored first to identify some of the basic modes of variation in theoretical orientation in psychology. I then looked for correlates of these dimensions in the hope of finding personal characteristics and life circumstances that accompany particular patterns of orientation—perhaps characteristics and circumstances that lead an individual to choose one theoretical position in preference to another. This hope has been realized to some extent.

There are obviously many possible modes of variation in theoretical orientation, but we have seen that these are describable to a great extent in terms of a small number of dimensions. At the same time, the determinants of theoretical orientation are quite numerous and subject to much variation from one individual to another, but there is reason to hope that we can find some systematic patterns of determination underlying positions in theory. It is reasonable to believe that discernible features of individual temperament and life history will temper receptivity to any given theoretical position and that certain kinds of people will tend to be drawn to any given theoretical camp and other types will be drawn elsewhere. It is unreasonable, however, to expect anything approaching a clear one-to-one relationship between theoretical orientation and either personality traits or life-history variables. We know that such determinants may be overridden by the accidents of university training. We know, too, that some psychologists undergo major shifts in orientation in the course of their careers without necessarily undergoing accompanying changes in personality. Some of these shifts probably serve to "correct" for the accidents of training and bring theoretical position more in line with personal disposition, but there is no good reason to assume that this is always the case.

In the present quest for the concomitants of theoretical orientation, our attention has centered mostly on two basic dimensions—objectivism vs. subjectivism and endogenism vs. exogenism—that have appeared in factor analyses both of ratings applied to major theorists and of questionnaire responses obtained from representative samples of contemporary psychologists. In the analyses of questionnaire data, objectivism can be seen to encompass a number of semi-independent components. These include:

1. Factual orientation: An inclination to espouse a radical empiricism and disparage speculation, abstract interpretation, and theory-building.
2. Impersonal causality: The advocacy of a determinism that excludes or de-emphasizes individual choice or participation.
3. Behavioral content emphasis: A tendency to focus on publicly observable behavior as subject matter and to consider this the appropriate subject matter for psychology.
4. Elementarism: A preference for dealing both in theory and research with relatively elementary or specific variables and relationships.
5. Physicalism: The view that psychologists should employ concepts definable in physical terms and seek laws and principles expressable in physical terms.
6. Quantitative orientation: A tendency to favor quantitative measurement, quantitative description, and the use of mathematical formulations in theory.

The third of these ingredients is probably the most central one, while the first and the sixth are relatively peripheral. In contrast, subjectivism is characterized by the following components:

1. Theoretical orientation: An inclination to favor theory-building and speculation that goes beyond the limits of extant observation.
2. Personal will: An emphasis on the importance of individual choice, purpose, and uniqueness and a tendency to regard these as necessary ingredients of any adequate explanation of human actions.
3. Experiential content emphasis: A tendency to regard the conscious experience of the individual as an essential subject matter for psychological theory and research.
4. Holism: A preference for dealing in both theory and research with complex global patterns and relationships.
5. A rejection of physicalism: An acceptance of terms and theoretical formulations that are not totally reducible to physical terms.

6. Qualitative orientation: A de-emphasis of quantitative procedures and formulations and an acceptance of subject matter and methods that do not readily permit quantitative treatment.

The dimension I have called endogenism vs. exogenism is concerned with a tendency to emphasize either the internal, biological sources or the external, environmental sources of human behavior and of individual differences in human behavior. We may distinguish two semi-independent components of this dimension—biological determinism and environmental determinism. The endogenist attaches more importance to the former than to the latter, while the exogenist does the opposite.

Of these two broad dimensions, objectivism vs. subjectivism is the more important, for it encompasses many more of the variations in theoretical positions that we see in psychology. It corresponds roughly to a division in outlook that has long distinguished people in the natural sciences from people in the arts and humanities. It approximates the contemporary division in psychology between behaviorists and humanistic psychologists. I have described it as a central expression of a still broader dimension that I have called restrictive vs. fluid orientation. The restrictive orientation rests on a basic predisposition to deal with reality in a relatively controlling and compartmental fashion. To achieve order and control, the restrictive individual may confine his attention to a narrow range of entities and events and insist on orderly observational procedures and orderly description. The fluid individual displays less insistence on order and is inclined to deal with people and life in all their complexity.

Both the objectivism-subjectivism dichotomy and the more comprehensive restrictive-fluid dimension correspond rather well to a few grand polarities in outlook that others have described and viewed as based on differences in temperament. The best known of these is William James' classification of philosophers into tough-minded and tender-minded types.[5] While James saw the division as basically one of temperament, he did not attempt to spell out the traits involved. His terms carry a heavy load of obvious connotation, however, and psychologists have found it easy to apply these terms to one another, along with an assortment of equivalent epithets (soft-headed, hard-nosed, etc.). The Jamesian dichotomy has been resurrected in a modern and still more colorful guise by Alan Watts, who has suggested that all major philosophical disputes entail an argument between the partisans of "prickles" and the partisans of "goo." He characterizes the "prickly" philosophers as tough-minded, rigorous, precise, and inclined to stress differences and divisions between things. On the other hand, "the gooey people are tender-minded romanticists who love wide generalizations and grand syntheses."[6]

Descriptions of this sort cry out for us to recognize a temperamental source for variations in theoretical outlook, and we have considered some research designed to illuminate this source. What can we say at this point about the life circumstances and personal characteristics that lead different psycholgists to choose differing intellectual positions? Let us consider first the dimension of objectivism-subjectivism. In some respects, this dimension parallels a division between Western culture and Eastern culture, as well as a division between Anglo-American culture and continental European culture. Anglo-American psychology is more objectivistic than continental European psychology. There is some evidence of broad cultural differences in family backgrounds between objectivists and subjectivists. The latter are more likely to show evidence of some influence from European sources. Objectivists are a little more likely to reject religion. Subjectivists are more likely to value religion and a little more likely to be Jewish.

It is possible that subjectivists are more likely to have experienced a lack of accord with American society, but objectivists are more likely to have experienced discord within their families. They more often report difficulties in their relationships with a parent, usually the parent of their own sex. They are also more likely than subjectivists to see their fathers as rather demanding or controlling. Thus, the concern of the objectivist for achieving and maintaining control in his intellectual work may have its roots in a childhood in which a fair amount of control was imposed on him and demanded of him. Objectivists are also a little more likely to have experienced sensory and motor handicaps as children, and these handicaps may have predisposed some of them to view human problems in physical terms.

Objectivism and subjectivism are accompanied by patterns of interests and values that affect intellectual perspectives with respect to a domain that extends far beyond the boundaries of psychology. The objectivist tends to have a relatively strong interest in such fields as physical science, engineering, and mathematics. The subjectivist tends to have a relatively strong interest in the arts and humanities. With respect to professional activities, the objectivist tends to have a stronger interest in research and is more likely to hold an academic position. The subjectivist is likely to have a stronger interest in psychotherapy or counseling. The objectivist has relatively strong theoretical and economic values, while the subjectivist is likely to have stronger aesthetic and social values.

The objectivist is more likely to hold science and the scientific method in high esteem. He is more likely to look to science for the solution of all sorts of problems, and he tends to accept many traditional values associated with science. Thus, the objectivist favors a kind of detachment and may attempt to understand people in much the same way he would understand a set of events involving inanimate objects and events. In dealing with people, the objectivist tends to be more object-oriented, while the subjectivist tends to be more person-oriented. The objectivist seeks to understand people in terms of a relatively limited set of characteristics. The subjectivist sees people in a more complex way and is aware of more ways in which they differ from one another.

The objectivist is oriented more to the concrete world. The subjectivist is oriented more to the psychological or subjective realm and is open to much more variation within his own conscious experience. We can describe many of the differences we see rather simply in Jungian terms. The objectivist tends to emphasize the functions of thinking and sensation, while the subjectivist tends to emphasize the functions of feeling and intuition. The objectivist strives to find well-defined truths, and to find them he emphasizes careful observation and description of concrete events and orderly, rational procedures. The subjectivist is more attuned to the realm of feeling and imagination, more accepting of vague, global descriptions, and more inclined to deal with intangible, symbolic meanings.

The evidence for personal and life-history correlates of the endogenism-exogenism dimension is less clear, and it is possible that one's position on this dimension is governed somewhat less by variations in temperament. The clearest findings point to a relationship to social introversion-extraversion. The endogenist is more likely to have come from a relatively protective and indulgent family environment and is more likely to have suffered from shyness as a child. The exogenist is more likely to have experienced difficulties stemming from his own aggressive behavior. The exogenist is likely to have been more physically active generally and to have devoted much time to active games and sports. The endogenist is more likely to have avoided this activity and to have disliked physical education during his school years. The endogenist tends to describe himself as quiet, reserved, and inaccessible. The exogenist tends to see himself as more talkative, expressive, and gregarious. Perhaps the endogenist tends to look for internal sources of behavior because he himself is relatively self-contained and insulated from the environment, while the exogenist interacts more freely and sees more of his actions as arising in interaction with others.

There is then some evidence that variations in theoretical orientation in psychology have some roots in personal temperament, and I have attempted to sketch a global picture that captures the strongest trends evident in my data. At best, we can account for only a fraction of the variance discernible in theoretical orientation. With different procedures and improved measuring instruments, we will be able to account for more. The psychology of psychology is still a new area of research, and much work remains to be done.

Appendix

The Theoretical Orientation Survey (TOS)

The Theoretical Orientation Survey is a 63-item inventory that contains scales for the following eight factors:

1. Factual (vs. theoretical) orientation
2. Impersonal causality (vs. personal will)
3. Behavioral (vs. experiential) content emphasis
4. Elementarism (vs. holism)
5. Biological determinism
6. Environmental determinism
7. Physicalism
8. Quantitative (vs. qualitative) orientation

By combining scores on these scales, one can obtain scores for two second-order factors:

I. Objectivism (vs. subjectivism)
II. Endogenism (vs. exogenism)

To take the inventory, a subject must have a question booklet and an answer sheet. For all items, a five-point Likert response scale is used, with the categories *strongly disagree, disagree, cannot say, agree,* and *strongly agree.* On the answer sheets that have been employed thus far in research with the TOS, these five terms have been printed as column headings. Below them, directly to the right of each item number, are the symbols *SD, D, ?, A,* and *SA.* The subject responds to each item by marking the appropriate symbol. The inventory itself is presented in the question booklet with initial marking instructions:

Theoretical Orientation Survey. The statements below represent a wide range of issues pertaining to theory and methods in psychology. Please indicate the extent of your agreement or disagreement with each one by drawing a line through the appropriate alternative on the answer form. Strictly speaking there are no right or wrong answers; your answers should reflect your own personal attitudes and inclinations. You may feel that some of the items are vague, obscure, or improperly stated, but try to decide in each case whether you agree or disagree with the item. Use the *cannot say* category no more than necessary.

1. A science is likely to progress most rapidly if researchers devote themselves primarily to the systematic gathering of factual information and engage in little elaborate speculation or theory building.

2. Human behavior is characterized in all aspects by lawful regularity and thus, in principle, it is completely predictable.

3. All behavior, except for a few simple reflexes, is learned.

4. Psychologists should be as concerned with explaining private conscious experience as they are with explaining overt behavior.

5. For many research purposes, it is best to permit many relevant variables to interact in a natural fashion and then analyze the results, rather than try to effect strict control.

6. Individual differences in personality are governed to a high degree by heredity.

7. All the concepts used in psychological theory should be explicitly definable in terms of observed physical events.

8. The use of mathematical models and equations in theory often serves to create a false impression of scientific respectability, instead of furthering our understanding.

9. It is just as important for psychological researchers to formulate theoretical interpretations as it is to accumulate specific facts about behavior.

10. In principle, human behavior cannot be completely predicted, because people can choose to act in ways that we have no basis for expecting.

11. Except for a few elementary drives like hunger and thirst, all human motives are learned.

12. The individual subject's personal account of his private conscious experience is one of the most valuable sources of psychological data.

13. Highly controlled experiments often give a misleading picture of the complex interactions that actually occur under natural circumstances.

14. The direction of human behavior is governed to a considerable extent by inborn predispositions.

15. It is best to define *perception* just in terms of stimulus-response relationships, rather than in terms of internal events that cannot be publicly observed.

16. Elaborate forms of statistical analysis tend to be over-emphasized in psychology.

17. A theory should consist mainly of inductive generalizations based on observations, with little in the way of contructions or hypothetical formulations contributed by the theorist.

18. Human actions are just as strictly determined by whatever causes are operating as all other physical events are.

19. Nearly all individual differences in human behavior can be accounted for in terms of past reinforcements.

20. Psychologists can gain many valuable insights through meditation and other procedures designed to expand or illuminate private experience.

21. In the long run researchers can achieve most if they devote each individual study to a very specific, circumscribed problem.

22. Much of the variation in human temperament is governed by inborn constitution.

23. Any meaningful statement about mental events can be translated into a statement about behavior with no serious loss of meaning.

24. Psychological theory could benefit greatly from more extensive use of mathematical and geometric models.

25. The most valuable theories are ones involving speculation that goes well beyond established facts and points the way to future discoveries.

26. In principle, an individual's choice or decision can never be fully predicted from antecedent conditions or events.

27. Nearly all the behavioral tendencies that have been called instinctive in people are actually products of learning.

28. The primary goal of psychologists should be the explanation of observable behavior, rather than the explanation of conscious events.

29. We would gain more valuable information if researchers spent more time studying total action patterns in relation to the total influencing environment and less time relating single responses to a few specific stimuli.

30. An individual's pattern of relative strengths and weaknesses in verbal, mathematical, and perceptual abilities is governed to a great extent by genetic factors.

31. As far as possible, the stimulus and response variables used in psychological theory should be defined in strictly physical terms.

32. Mathematical equations are not a very appropriate device for expressing the most fundamental relationships and principles in psychological theory.

33. Most of the important landmarks in the history of any science are empirical discoveries, not theories.

34. Human behavior is not completely predictable, because people are too individually unique.

35. Every feature of human behavior is susceptible to extensive modification by learning.

36. A present, there is as great a need in psychological research for sensitive, introspective observers as for refinements in design and instrumentation.

37. Our most important information in psychology is obtained by well-controlled experiments in which we systematically vary one or a few independent variables and record their effects on a specific dependent variable.

38. Individual differences in biochemical constitution underlie much important variation in behavior.

39. All the concepts used in psychological theory should be explicitly definable in terms of operations of observation and measurement.

40. Many of the most important relationships in psychology can best be examined by complex kinds of statistical analysis.

41. Single, isolated facts and findings are of little value until they are related to other facts and findings by theoretical interpretation.

42. Strictly speaking, there are no random or chance events, since all events are characterized by lawful regularities.

43. Every frequently recurring action is controlled or regulated to a great extent by environmental influences or effects, whether the individual who displays it realizes this or not.

44. Psychologists should devote more effort to explaining observable behavior than to explaining conscious experience.

45. Psychologists often get their best insights from research activities in which they do not try to achieve careful measurement or quantification.

46. There are marked hereditary differences among people in susceptibility to mental illness.

47. In scientific writing, psychologists should either avoid making statements about conscious phenomena or try to translate such statement into statements about physical conditions and events.

48. As this science progresses, psychological theories will tend increasingly to be composed of abstract mathematical or logical equations.

49. Science can best advance if theorists are willing to speculate freely beyond the limits of currently available evidence.

50. In principle, we could predict all of a person's behavior if we had complete knowledge of his physiological condition and of the events that had previously occurred in his life.

51. Higher mental processes are largely products of learning.

52. All aspects of conscious human experience should be considered appropriate subject matter for psychology.

53. The explanation of behavior in complex social systems probably requires the use of principles that are not manifested in interactions within small groups.

54. Many of the behavioral differences between men and women are a function of inherent biological differences between the sexes.

55. It is best to define *learning* just in terms of a change in response, without any reference to events that cannot be publicly observed.

56. A strong insistence on precise measurement and quantification is likely to cause psychologists to neglect important areas of research.

57. When general theories are constructed before much systematic research has been done in an area, they tend to impede scientific progress.

58. The experience of personal choice is actually an illusion.

59. Individual differences in personality are mostly a pro-

duct of environmental influence.

60. Psychologists should strive to develop a more elaborate and precise vocabulary for describing conscious emotional states and other qualities of experience.

61. Psychologists should undertake more studies of broad scope, aimed at charting major areas of investigation, before proceeding to test so many specific hypotheses.

62. The structure of human thought is governed to a great extent by innate factors.

63. A good indicator of the maturity of a science is the extent to which its explanatory principles are stated in a precise quantitative form.

SCORING

The following key indicates which items are scored for each of the first-order factor scales and the direction of scoring of each item:

Factor 1	Factor 2	Factor 3	Factor 4
1. +	2. +	4. −	5. −
9. −	10. −	12. −	13. −
17. +	18. +	20. −	21. +
25. −	26. −	28. +	29. −
33. +	34. −	36. −	37. +
41. −	42. +	44. +	45. −
49. −	50. +	52. −	53. −
57. +	58. +	60. −	61. −
Factor 5	Factor 6	Factor 7	Factor 8
6. +	3. +	7. +	8. −
14. +	11. +	15. +	16. −
22. +	19. +	23. +	24. +
30. +	27. +	31. +	32. −
38. +	35. +	39. +	40. +
46. +	43. +	47. +	48. +
54. +	51. +	55. +	56. −
62. +	59. +		63. +

The total score for any scale is a sum of item weights. For each positive item, the item alternatives are weighted as follows: SD = 1, D = 2, ? = 3, A = 4, SA = 5. For negative items, the weights run in the reverse direction: SD = 5, D = 4, ? = 3, A = 2, SA = 1. If scoring is to be done by hand, one can expedite the process by preparing a separate stencil key for each scale. An easy way of doing this is to use an answer sheet for each stencil and to cut out the row of symbols (SD-D-?-A-SA) for each of the seven or eight items to be scored, then to write in the item weights in proper sequence above the openings in the sheet. If this sheet is placed over a marked answer sheet, one can rapidly obtain a scale score by simply adding the weights that correspond to the marks that appear.

The scoring formulas for the second-order factors are as follows:

$$F_I = F_2 + F_3 + F_4 + F_7 + F_8$$

$$F_{II} = 50 + F_5 - F_6$$

In other words, to obtain a score for the factor I (objectivism vs. subjectivism), we would simply add together the scores for factors 2, 3, 4, 7, and 8. To obtain a score for factor II (endogenism vs. exogenism), we would add the score for factor 5 to a constant of 50 and subtract the score for factor 6.

NORMATIVE DATA

Means and standard deviations were computed for the orientation scales on the basis of data provided by 866 APA members who agreed to complete the inventory. These values were calculated not only for all the full scales, but also for the abbreviated scales obtained by using only the first 32 items of the inventory. The total sample contained 510 men and 356 women. Values for the total sample are shown in Table A. Values for the male and female subsamples are given in Tables B and C.

Notes

Chapter 1

1. K. B. Madsen. *Theories of motivation*. Kent, Ohio: Kent State University Press, 1968.
2. Richard W. Coan. "Toward a psychological interpretation of psychology." *Journal of the History of the Behavioral Sciences,* 1973, 9, 313–327. The remainder of this chapter is essentially an expansion of the material presented in the first half of that paper.
3. Melvin H. Marx and William A. Hillix. *Systems and theories in psychology*. New York: McGraw-Hill, 1973.
4. See Richard W. Coan. "Theoretical concepts in psychology." *British Journal of Statistical Psychology,* 1964, 17, 161–176.
5. Ernst Cassirer. *The philosophy of symbolic forms*. New Haven: Yale University Press, 1953.
6. These concepts are developed in numerous works of Piaget. For an excellent summary of Piaget's theoretical contributions, see John H. Flavell. *The developmental psychology of Jean Piaget*. New York: Van Nostrand, 1963.
7. Richard W. Coan. "Facts, factors, and artifacts: the quest for psychological meaning." *Psychological Review,* 1964, 71, 123–140.
8. Abraham H. Maslow. *The psychology of science: a reconaissance*. New York: Harper & Row, 1966.
9. Carl G. Jung. *The basic writings of C. G. Jung*. New York: Random House, 1959. p. 317.
10. Benjamin L. Whorf. *Collected papers on metalinguistics*. Washington: Foreign Service Institute, Department of State, 1952.
11. Norbert Wiener. *Cybernetics, or control and communication in the animal and the machine*. New York: Wiley, 1948.
12. Ludwig von Bertalanffy. *General system theory: foundations, development, applications*. New York: George Braziller, 1968.
13. Claude E. Shannon and Warren Weaver. *The mathematical theory of communication*. Urbana: University of Illinois Press, 1964.
14. Stephen C. Pepper. *World hypotheses*. Berkeley: University of California Press, 1966.
15. *General system theory*.

Chapter 2

1. Liam Hudson. *Frames of mind: ability, perception and self-perception in the arts and sciences*. New York: Norton, 1970.
2. C. P. Snow. *The two cultures and a second look: an expanded version of the two cultures and the scientific revolution*. Cambridge: Cambridge University Press, 1964.

3. Joseph R. Royce. *The encapsulated man: an interdisciplinary essay on the search for meaning*. New York: Van Nostrand Reinhold, 1964.
4. Anne Roe. *The making of a scientist*. New York: Dodd, Mead, and Company, 1953. Also Anne Roe. "A psychological study of eminent psychologists and anthropologists, and a comparison with biological and physical scientists." *Psychological Monographs*, 1953, 67 (2, Whole No. 352).
5. M. D. Galinsky. "Personality development and vocational choice: a study of physicists and clinical psychologists." Unpublished doctoral dissertation, University of Michigan, 1961.
6. R. B. Cattell and J. E. Drevdahl. "A comparison of the personality profile (16P.F.) of eminent researchers with that of eminent teachers and administrators, and of the general population." *British Journal of Psychology*, 1955, 46, 248–261.
7. J. E. Drevdahl and R. B. Cattell. "Personality and creativity in artists and writers." *Journal of Clinical Psychology*, 1958, 14, 107–111.
8. Carl R. Rogers. "Two divergent trends." In Rollo May (Ed.) *Existential psychology*. New York: Random House, 1961.
9. Gordon W. Allport. *Becoming: basic considerations for a psychology of personality*. New Haven: Yale University Press, 1955.
10. H. L. Ansbacher. "On the origin of holism." *Journal of Individual Psychology*, 1961, 17, 142–148.
11. Henry A. Murray. *Explorations in personality*. New York: Oxford University Press, 1938.
12. William James. *Pragmatism*. London: Longmans, Green, 1907.
13. Egon Brunswik. "The conceptual framework of psychology." *International encyclopedia of unified science*, Vol. 1, No. 10. Chicago: University of Chicago Press, 1952.
14. Robert I. Watson. "Psychology: a prescriptive science." *American Psychologist*, 1967, 22, 435–443.
15. This analysis is reported in Richard W. Coan. "Dimensions of psychological theory." *American Psychologist*, 1968, 23, 715–722.
16. Richard W. Coan and Salvatore V. Zagona. "Contemporary ratings of psychological theorists." *Psychological Record*, 1962, 12, 315–322.

Chapter 3
1. I have discussed issues relating to the generality level of factors in Richard W. Coan. "Facts, factors, and artifacts: the quest for psychological meaning." *Psychological Review*, 1964, 71, 123–140.

Chapter 4
1. Richard W. Coan. "Child personality and developmental psychology." In Raymond B. Cattell (Ed.) *Handbook of multivariate experimental psychology*. Chicago: Rand McNally, 1966. pp. 732–752. Also Richard W. Coan. "The changing personality." In Ralph Mason Dreger (Ed.) *Multivariate personality research: contributions to the understanding of personality in honor of Raymond B. Cattell*. Baton Rouge: Claitor's Publishing Division, 1972. pp. 352–386.
2. Jerome S. Bruner and Gordon W. Allport. "Fifty years of change in American psychology." *Psychological Bulletin*, 1940, 37, 757–776.
3. S. W. Fernberger. "The scientific interests and scientific publications of the members of the American Psychological Association." *Psychological Bulletin*, 1938, 35, 261–281.
4. Gordon W. Allport. "The psychologist's frame of reference." *Psychological*

Bulletin, 1940, 37, 1–28, p. 5.

5. Egon Brunswik. "The conceptual framework of psychology." *International encyclopedia of unified science,* Vol. 1, No. 10. Chicago: University of Chicago Press, 1952.

6. K. B. Madsen. *Theories of motivation.* Kent, Ohio: Kent State University Press, 1968.

7. Thomas S. Kuhn. "The structure of scientific revolutions." *International encyclopedia of unified science,* Vol. 2, No. 2. Chicago: University of Chicago Press, 1970.

8. Richard W. Coan. *The optimal personality: an empirical and theoretical analysis.* New York: Columbia University Press, 1974.

9. Albert R. Gilgen. "Converging trends in psychology." Paper presented at convention of American Psychological Association, 1974.

10. Sigmund Koch. "Psychology as an integral discipline: the history of an illusion" and "Conceptual sweep vs. knowledge: thoughts towards a feasible future for psychology." Papers presented at convention of American Psychological Association, 1974.

11. D. O. Hebb. "What psychology is all about." *American Psychologist,* 1974, 29, 71–79.

Chapter 5

1. While I assembled this myself, I borrowed quite heavily from the biographical questionnaire of Roe and Siegelman, which is reported in Anne Roe and Marvin Siegelman. *The origin of interests.* Washington, D. C.: American Personnel and Guidance Association, 1964.

2. Anne Roe and Marvin Siegelman. "A parent-child relations questionnaire." *Child Development,* 1963, 34, 355–369.

3. Leonard V. Gordon. *Manual for Survey of Interpersonal Values.* Chicago: Science Research Associates, 1960.

4. R. B. Cattell, D. R. Saunders, and G. Stice. *Handbook for the Sixteen Personality Factor Questionnaire.* Champaign, Illinois: Institute for Personality and Ability Testing, 1957.

5. See Richard W. Coan, Marcia T. Fairchild, and Zipporah P. Dobyns. "Dimensions of experienced control." *Journal of Social Psychology,* 1973, 91, 53–60. See also Richard W. Coan. *The optimal personality: an empirical and theoretical analysis.* New York: Columbia University Press, 1974. This book covers the work done with the preliminary version of the Personal Opinion Survey.

6. Isabel Briggs Myers. *Manual: The Myers-Briggs Type Indicator.* Princeton, New Jersey: Educational Testing Service, 1962.

7. Richard W. Coan. "Measurable components of openness to experience." *Journal of Consulting and Clinical Psychology,* 1972, 39, 346. See also *The optimal personality.*

8. Gordon W. Allport, Philip E. Vernon, and Gardner Lindzey. *Manual: Study of Values.* New York: Houghton Mifflin, 1970.

9. Richard W. Coan, Richard W. Hanson, and Zipporah P. Dobyns. "The development of some factored scales of general beliefs." *Journal of Social Psychology,* 1972, 86, 161–62. See also *The optimal personality.*

10. J. R. Royce. *Manual: Psycho-Epistemological Profile.* Edmonton: Department of Psychology, University of Alberta, 1970.

11 Linda C. Wyrick. "Relationships between theoretical orientation, therapeutic orientation, and personal involvement with patients." Unpublished doctoral dissertation, University of Arizona, 1971.

Chapter 6
1. See *The optimal personality.*

Chapter 7
1. Leonard V. Gordon. *Manual for Survey of Interpersonal Values.* Chicago: Science Research Associates, 1960. p. 3.
2. The development of this questionnaire is discussed briefly in Richard W. Coan, Richard W. Hanson, and Zipporah P. Dobyns. "The development of some factored scales of general beliefs." *Journal of Social Psychology,* 1972, 86, 161–162. See also *The optimal personality.*
3. Marjorie Ann Crago. "The relationship between theoretical orientation and complexity-simplicity among psychologists." Unpublished doctoral dissertation, University of Arizona, 1974.
4. Joseph R. Royce. *The encapsulated man: an interdisciplinary essay on the search for meaning.* New York: Van Nostrand Reinhold, 1964.
5. See *The optimal personality.*

Chapter 8
1. The development of the Experience Inventory is described in *The optimal personality.*
2. The development of this instrument is also described in *The optimal personality.* See also Richard W. Coan, Marcia T. Fairchild, and Zipporah P. Dobyns. "Dimensions of experienced control." *Journal of Social Psychology,* 1973, 91, 53–60.
3. See Isabel Briggs Myers. *Manual: The Myers-Briggs Type Indicator.* Princeton, New Jersey: Educational Testing Service, 1962.
4. Carl G. Jung. *Psychological types.* New York: Harcourt, 1933.
5. I have discussed this matter at somewhat greater length elsewhere. See Richard W. Coan. *Hero, artist, sage, and saint.* New York: Columbia University Press, 1977. See also Ira Progoff. *The death and rebirth of psychology.* New York: McGraw-Hill, 1956. For a more detailed account of the development of these theorists, see Henri F. Ellenberger. *The discovery of the unconscious.* New York: Basic Books, 1970.
6. Ernest Jones. *The life and work of Sigmund Freud.* New York: Basic Books, 1961.

Chapter 9
1. C. G. Jung. *Memories, dreams, reflections.* New York: Vintage Books, 1963. p. 21.
2. From the autobiography of John Broadus Watson in Carl Murchison (Ed.) *A history of psychology in autobiography. Volume III.* Worcester: Clark University Press, 1936. p. 271.
3. From the autobiography of Carl Rogers in Edwin G. Boring and Gardner Lindzey (Eds.) *A history of psychology in autobiography. Volume V.* New York: Irvington Publishers, 1967. p. 345.
4. From the autobiography of B. F. Skinner in Edwin G. Boring and Gardner Lindzey (Eds.) *A history of psychology in autobiography. Volume V.* New York: Irvington Publishers, 1967. p. 388.
5. William James. *Pragmatism.* London: Longmans, Green, 1907.
6. Alan W. Watts. *The book on the taboo against knowing who you are.* New York: Collier Books, 1966.

Tables

Table 1. Alpha Reliability Coefficients

Factor	32-item inventory	40-item inventory	48-item inventory	56-item inventory	63-item inventory
1	.717	.747	.741	.765	.784
2	.804	.837	.842	.850	.856
3	.736	.783	.825	.833	.833
4	.618	.706	.733	.707	.733
5	.774	.793	.817	.815	.833
6	.793	.757	.751	.767	.788
7	.684	.748	.798	.818	.818*
8	.714	.738	.756	.762	.778
I	.845	.879	.897	.906	.914
II	.820	.819	.828	.832	.857

*Since there are only 7 items in the scale for factor 7, this value is necessarily the same as the corresponding value for the 56-item inventory.

Table 2. Retest Reliabilities

Factor	32-item inventory	40-item inventory	48-item inventory	56-item inventory	63-item inventory
1	.608	.623	.637	.665	.684
2	.809	.827	.840	.848	.860
3	.811	.807	.830	.834	.839
4	.684	.726	.767	.755	.767
5	.718	.754	.776	.792	.817
6	.761	.771	.781	.785	.805
7	.736	.780	.804	.822	.822*
8	.760	.772	.788	.802	.813
I	.881	.895	.910	.907	.908
II	.773	.793	.808	.814	.833

*Since there are only 7 items in the scale for Factor 7, this value is necessarily the same as the corresponding value for the 56-item inventory.

Table 3. Mean Factor Scores for Leading Theorists within Decades: 1880—1959

	Factor					
Decade	*1*	*2*	*3*	*4*	*5*	*6*
1880–1889	56.1	46.1	51.8	50.4	42.7	51.0
1890–1899	55.5	47.4	47.2	47.8	46.8	53.0
1900–1909	50.5	47.8	48.7	48.1	47.6	51.5
1910–1919	49.6	53.0	48.3	46.2	52.4	55.1
1920–1929	46.2	54.8	55.4	45.4	49.9	52.6
1930–1939	43.9	51.9	55.1	48.7	53.4	48.5
1940–1949	42.1	49.4	56.3	56.2	53.8	43.7
1950–1959	39.4	46.6	55.5	57.4	55.0	42.3

Table 4. Mean Ratings on Theoretical Variables for Leading Theorists within Decades: 1880—1959

	Decade							
Variable	1880–1889	1890–1899	1900–1909	1910–1919	1920–1929	1930–1939	1940–1949	1950–1959
1	2.62	2.77	2.89	2.92	3.15	3.49	3.46	3.73
2	3.38	3.05	2.86	2.67	2.95	2.65	2.78	2.78
3	2.52	2.68	2.83	3.10	3.03	3.29	3.35	3.36
4	3.28	3.29	2.78	2.64	2.68	2.44	2.38	2.28
5	2.90	2.89	3.18	3.19	3.35	3.59	3.64	3.65
6	2.38	2.42	2.02	2.40	2.11	2.00	1.97	1.96
7	2.56	2.94	2.94	2.92	2.80	2.71	2.70	2.86
8	2.31	2.44	2.23	2.46	2.35	2.23	2.22	2.19
9	2.66	2.85	3.10	2.99	2.96	2.87	2.70	2.75
10	2.26	2.56	2.54	2.69	2.66	2.81	2.85	2.86
11	2.50	2.54	2.71	2.59	2.34	2.41	2.29	2.23
12	2.86	3.06	3.09	3.10	2.96	3.21	3.03	3.40
13	3.00	2.79	3.00	2.93	3.30	3.32	3.34	3.33
14	2.51	2.56	2.61	2.90	3.07	2.95	2.95	2.76
15	2.31	2.35	2.28	2.54	2.54	2.40	2.27	2.26
16	2.33	2.47	2.49	2.82	2.56	2.53	2.37	2.29
17	3.36	3.31	2.71	2.49	2.37	2.00	1.67	1.58
18	2.94	2.57	2.76	2.40	2.65	2.88	3.37	3.50
19	2.48	2.17	2.07	2.02	2.01	2.37	2.78	2.87
20	2.63	2.71	2.38	2.49	2.35	2.17	1.94	1.89
21	2.66	2.70	2.75	2.86	2.88	2.68	2.45	2.44
22	2.20	2.11	1.81	1.86	1.49	1.35	1.35	1.30
23	2.94	2.99	3.11	2.98	3.20	3.39	3.22	3.35
24	1.84	1.90	1.82	2.11	1.80	1.64	1.53	1.44
25	2.50	2.22	2.38	2.24	2.49	2.66	2.66	2.59
26	2.31	2.09	2.32	2.25	2.42	2.91	3.38	3.39
27	2.93	2.56	2.72	1.98	1.76	2.12	2.26	2.52

28	2.19	2.16	2.18	2.31	2.48	2.52	2.31	2.19
29	3.12	3.02	3.15	3.30	3.32	3.26	3.38	3.38
30	2.73	2.51	2.62	2.40	2.15	2.32	2.58	2.60
31	2.97	2.43	2.33	2.19	2.24	2.53	2.93	2.90
32	2.63	2.32	2.34	2.21	2.28	2.56	2.88	2.87
33	2.66	3.00	2.94	3.22	3.20	3.20	3.21	3.03
34	2.48	2.19	2.24	2.48	2.88	2.67	2.69	2.39

Table 5. Scores for Theorists on Six Factors of Theoretical Orientation

| | | | Factor | | | |
Theorist	1	2	3	4	5	6
1. S. Freud	51	51	40	30	63	73
2. C. L. Hull	34	38	64	59	57	38
3. W. Wundt	57	38	56	57	32	42
4. I. P. Pavlov	27	38	57	61	43	55
5. J. B. Watson	25	39	58	56	51	39
6. E. L. Thorndike	39	42	51	55	54	49
7. W. James	55	61	46	44	61	56
8. M. Wertheimer	55	66	61	36	35	53
9. E. C. Tolman	45	58	58	59	57	47
10. K. Lewin	50	65	57	49	55	42
11. W. Köhler	56	68	68	37	42	58
12. H. von Helmholtz	53	39	56	55	39	55
13. B. F. Skinner	30	38	61	55	48	23
14. J. Dewey	57	59	45	41	59	48
15. K. Koffka	58	67	69	37	43	55
16. K. S. Lashley	39	52	61	52	47	56
17. E. B. Titchener	59	34	61	45	30	36
18. J. Piaget	61	58	48	38	53	53
19. D. O. Hebb	41	46	55	59	58	59
20. W. McDougall	66	67	41	41	67	66
21. G. T. Fechner	61	44	60	61	34	44
22. L. L. Thurstone	46	41	45	72	47	52
23. A. Binet	51	48	31	65	39	54
24. H. Ebbinghaus	48	36	55	65	36	36
25. C. E. Spearman	49	43	42	70	37	44
26. C. S. Sherrington	38	46	57	43	39	56
27. G. W. Allport	60	67	36	42	59	51
28. F. Galton	52	46	42	60	41	75
29. E. R. Guthrie	35	40	55	49	52	48
30. C. G. Jung	66	56	33	35	66	68
31. C. R. Rogers	57	65	40	43	58	38
32. N. E. Miller	33	43	55	62	60	42
33. A. Adler	62	60	32	41	66	46
34. R. S. Woodworth	52	49	53	53	55	53
35. K. W. Spence	29	32	60	67	56	38

36. E. Brunswik	49	56	53	55	48	48
37. W. B. Cannon	45	49	54	49	46	65
38. P. Janet	61	56	35	30	53	52
39. O. H. Mowrer	52	47	54	44	65	41
40. F. Brentano	63	56	46	39	39	39
41. H. F. Harlow	35	46	55	56	56	49
42. O. Külpe	54	43	53	52	37	44
43. J. M. Charcot	55	51	37	34	59	58
44. K. Goldstein	60	72	41	33	49	57
45. K. Horney	55	55	40	41	57	46
46. H. Rorschach	60	53	30	51	55	52
47. L. M. Terman	50	48	34	69	45	56
48. H. S. Sullivan	55	55	42	36	64	42
49. J. McK. Cattell	48	46	47	57	45	55
50. E. Mach	58	47	59	43	33	50
51. G. S. Hall	61	50	39	54	56	68
52. G. E. Müller	59	43	61	46	53	55
53. J. R. Angell	60	55	48	38	50	36
54. W. K. Estes	23	35	64	74	44	38

Table 6. Correlations between Psychological Interest Areas and Eight Factors of Theoretical Orientation

	Factor							
Interest area	1	2	3	4	5	6	7	8
1	.16	.29	.30	.29	.05	.15	.22	.13
2	−.29	−.11	−.20	−.20	.19	−.14	−.27	.05
3	.11	−.02	.05	.15	.16	.02	.03	.15
4	−.18	−.17	−.23	−.12	.06	.00	−.24	.08
5	−.13	−.05	−.08	−.04	−.01	.04	−.05	−.05
6	.34	.41	.44	.42	.21	−.04	.33	.13
7	.18	.12	.14	.19	.21	−.04	.07	.10
8	.14	−.05	.04	.08	.21	−.14	.04	.08
9	−.19	−.27	−.27	−.19	−.01	−.07	−.22	−.22
10	−.22	−.18	−.34	−.26	−.15	.04	−.33	−.26
11	−.12	−.16	−.30	−.23	−.14	.06	−.23	−.25
12	−.24	−.38	−.45	−.36	−.11	.02	−.36	−.13
13	−.35	−.36	−.50	−.46	−.11	−.07	−.42	−.25
14	−.29	−.27	−.44	−.43	−.18	.01	−.27	−.16
15	−.32	−.22	−.43	−.39	−.14	.04	−.25	−.11
16	−.29	−.23	−.37	−.36	−.13	.09	−.26	−.05
17	−.23	−.14	−.21	−.18	.02	.04	−.23	−.02
18	−.07	−.17	−.31	−.23	.05	−.16	−.25	−.09
19	−.26	−.25	−.51	−.44	−.06	−.16	−.43	−.19
20	−.11	−.20	−.33	−.23	−.02	−.18	−.13	−.08
21	−.07	−.16	−.16	−.18	−.14	.14	−.03	−.09
22	.01	−.14	−.12	−.14	−.09	.14	−.03	.10
23	.07	.04	.00	.09	.07	−.02	−.04	.10
24	−.16	.00	−.16	−.07	.02	−.14	−.15	−.03
25	.06	.03	.12	.16	.09	−.06	.14	.40

Table 7. Correlations between PCR Variables and Theoretical Orientation Factors for Men*

PCR form and variable	TOS factor									
	1	*2*	*3*	*4*	*5*	*6*	*7*	*8*	*I*	*II*
Mother form										
Loving	.058	.081	−.095	.063	−.016	.079	−.047	.051	.012	−.053
Demanding	−.146	.022	.114	−.066	.156	.005	.163	.110	.093	.087
Attentive	−.209	−.144	−.193	−.126	.267	−.132	−.213	−.022	−.184	.288
Rejecting	−.031	−.109	.076	−.109	−.027	.014	.039	−.021	−.030	−.023
Casual	.147	.020	−.144	.025	−.095	−.060	−.058	−.110	−.067	−.022
Loving-rejecting	.031	.102	−.097	.091	.022	.008	−.056	.025	.015	.009
Casual-demanding	.156	−.010	−.141	.041	−.135	−.016	−.123	−.111	−.090	−.070
Father form										
Loving	−.129	−.216	−.109	−.010	−.104	−.107	−.214	−.102	−.181	−.002
Demanding	.143	.148	.306	.184	.094	.061	.373	.177	.311	.021
Attentive	−.167	−.219	−.054	−.052	.161	−.186	−.088	−.003	−.118	.194
Rejecting	.224	.105	.106	.020	.175	.046	.262	.068	.154	.076
Casual	.005	−.142	−.236	−.126	.003	−.169	−.166	−.291	−.247	.094
Loving-rejecting	−.189	−.171	−.115	−.016	−.149	−.081	−.254	−.090	−.178	−.042
Casual-demanding	−.060	−.158	−.309	−.166	−.078	−.098	−.308	−.249	−.309	.008

*For an N of 75, coefficients of .228 and .296 would correspond respectively to the .05 and .01 levels of significance.

Table 8. Correlations between PCR Variables and Theoretical Orientation Factors for Women*

PCR form and variable	TOS factor									
	1	2	3	4	5	6	7	8	I	II
Mother form										
Loving	.139	-.057	.167	-.067	-.101	.157	.021	.093	.037	-.149
Demanding	.068	.234	-.004	.233	.144	.044	.191	-.063	.163	.061
Attentive	.117	-.032	.095	.163	.108	-.102	.039	-.116	.033	.122
Rejecting	-.101	.116	-.139	.154	.091	-.090	.104	.050	.079	.105
Casual	-.139	-.159	-.128	-.188	-.066	-.057	-.163	-.026	-.179	-.008
Loving-rejecting	.126	-.088	.160	-.113	-.101	.132	-.041	.025	-.019	-.134
Casual-demanding	-.114	-.216	-.064	-.230	-.119	-.050	-.194	.026	-.184	-.043
Father form										
Loving	-.137	-.067	.221	-.052	-.007	.157	.061	.282	.111	-.093
Demanding	.240	.250	.058	.148	.027	.163	.199	.011	.185	-.076
Attentive	.008	-.010	.026	.163	.025	-.091	.068	-.034	.051	.066
Rejecting	.094	.040	-.103	.081	-.082	-.080	.010	-.175	-.037	-.003
Casual	-.308	-.182	-.196	-.164	.026	-.194	-.149	-.049	-.200	.125
Loving-rejecting	-.120	-.056	.170	-.069	.038	.124	.028	.239	.078	-.048
Casual-demanding	-.294	-.245	-.137	-.171	.004	-.203	-.200	-.044	-.218	.117

*For an N of 83, coefficients of .216 and .281 would correspond respectively to the .05 and .01 levels of significance.

Table 9. Correlations between Childhood Problems and Theoretical Orientation Factors

Subject group and problem	Factor									
	1	2	3	4	5	6	7	8	I	II
Total sample (N=158)										
Shyness	-.082	-.026	-.167	-.010	.097	-.181	-.023	-.056	-.073	.159
Fights	-.093	.024	-.033	-.099	-.092	.147	.014	-.080	-.039	-.136
Fears	.063	.129	-.016	.144	-.080	-.007	.009	.136	.105	.051
Illness	-.035	-.067	-.096	-.153	.100	-.029	-.045	.035	-.084	.074
Handicap	.049	.185	.112	.163	.063	.059	.265	.066	.210	.004
Teacher clashes	-.009	-.018	.051	.024	-.079	.159	.058	-.002	.028	-.136
Total problems	-.062	.073	-.114	.003	.094	-.020	.061	.027	.017	.066
Men (N=75)										
Shyness	-.324	-.010	-.126	.056	.126	-.169	-.168	.117	-.045	.168
Fights	-.047	-.080	-.029	-.079	-.152	.222	.035	-.094	-.061	-.212
Fears	.135	.246	.077	.086	.158	.001	.058	.248	.188	.091
Illness	.076	.070	-.056	-.275	.028	.012	-.047	-.013	-.065	.010
Handicap	.131	.191	.169	.172	.072	.133	.295	.013	.224	-.032
Teacher clashes	.074	-.062	.085	.001	-.195	.276	.080	-.159	-.011	-.267
Total problems	-.043	.139	.013	-.013	.037	.123	.044	.072	.073	-.047
Women (N=83)										
Shyness	.095	-.093	-.273	-.102	.083	-.238	.059	-.229	-.173	.184
Fights	-.163	.133	-.055	-.131	-.024	.059	-.041	-.071	-.032	-.048
Fears	.048	.078	-.067	.220	.014	.015	.031	.069	.090	.000
Illness	-.125	-.187	-.130	-.046	.161	-.054	-.023	.081	-.091	.126
Handicap	-.067	.168	.020	.146	.057	-.036	.218	.120	.182	.056
Teacher clashes	-.177	.007	-.046	.027	.091	-.027	-.053	.196	.037	.069
Total problems	-.104	-.013	-.286	.005	.153	-.172	.057	-.023	-.069	.188

Table 10. Correlations between Theoretical Orientation Factors and Activities of Childhood and Adolescence*

Activity	1	2	3	4	5	6	7	8	I	II
					Factor					
Active games, sports	-.036	-.032	.044	.047	-.234	.175	.065	.008	.031	-.235
Reading	-.169	-.040	-.100	-.088	.081	-.070	-.202	.050	-.099	.087
Artwork	.115	.077	.084	-.048	.022	.060	.044	-.023	.042	-.021
Construction	.156	.104	.132	.067	-.018	.134	.104	-.094	.088	-.087
Collecting	.137	.066	.114	.153	.004	.120	.106	.011	.115	-.065
Music	-.014	-.141	-.043	-.014	.095	-.195	-.090	.088	-.062	.165
Talking	.010	-.006	-.006	.023	.003	.022	-.018	-.075	-.021	-.010
TV, radio, records	-.010	.032	-.025	.065	.058	-.061	-.066	-.069	-.016	.068
Club activities	-.060	.049	.037	.060	.008	.085	-.036	.082	.049	-.043
Dramatics	.094	.036	.066	.114	.065	-.094	.089	-.028	.071	.091

*$N = 158$. Hence, coefficients of .161 and .211 would correspond respectively to the .05 and .01 levels of significance.

Table 11. Correlations between Theoretical Orientation Factors and Academic Interests in College*

Academic area	Factor									
	1	2	3	4	5	6	7	8	I	II
Composition	-.066	-.023	-.129	-.162	.114	-.082	-.118	-.097	-.131	.113
Literature	.004	-.029	-.104	.008	.060	-.025	.031	-.031	-.034	.049
Foreign Languages	-.084	-.029	-.234	-.203	-.078	-.033	-.102	-.189	-.189	-.027
Mathematics	-.024	.105	.162	.076	.013	.164	.086	.172	.156	-.085
Social sciences	-.054	-.026	-.068	-.062	-.002	-.028	-.074	-.076	-.077	.015
Biology	.093	.106	.111	.167	.010	.064	.084	.092	.144	-.031
Physical sciences	-.005	.203	.158	.117	-.097	.152	.093	.171	.197	-.141
History	-.123	-.129	-.015	-.059	-.046	.024	-.062	-.002	-.077	-.041
Philosophy	.081	-.040	.023	.083	.004	-.071	.037	.028	.028	.042
Art	.059	-.090	-.040	-.061	-.064	-.008	-.063	-.132	-.101	-.032
Music	-.098	-.202	-.233	-.088	-.061	-.087	-.155	-.105	-.211	.014
Drama	.114	.009	-.040	.064	-.058	.081	.014	-.093	-.011	-.044
Physical education	.040	-.106	-.062	-.059	-.235	.175	-.086	-.114	-.113	-.236

*N = 158. Coefficients of .161 and .211 would correspond respectively to the .05 and .01 levels of significance.

Table 12. Correlations between Theoretical Orientation Factors and Occupational Interests*

Occupation	Factor									
	1	2	3	4	5	6	7	8	I	II
Artist	-.137	-.147	-.117	-.181	-.040	-.089	-.106	-.199	-.194	.027
Banker	.085	.007	.122	.051	.028	.140	.042	-.028	.050	-.063
Engineer	.202	.234	.237	.198	.052	.146	.203	.098	.257	-.052
Farmer	-.056	-.064	-.094	-.115	-.076	.130	-.055	-.027	-.091	-.118
Lawyer	.060	.104	.020	.089	.075	-.025	.051	.013	.075	.058
Mathematician	.070	.087	.180	.088	.065	.046	.116	.259	.186	.012
Minister	-.069	-.144	-.101	-.161	.046	.045	-.109	.018	-.133	.001
Musician	-.116	-.267	-.216	-.092	-.065	-.149	-.166	-.149	-.241	.046
Novelist	-.167	-.198	-.181	-.209	-.011	-.054	-.113	-.181	-.230	.024
Physical scientist	.025	.157	.150	.073	.034	.058	.078	.222	.178	-.013
Physician	-.093	-.180	-.121	-.082	.052	-.040	-.133	-.133	-.174	.053
Retail business owner	.117	-.004	.095	.076	.118	.037	.072	-.066	.043	.048
Salesman	-.118	-.098	-.158	-.020	.109	-.065	-.143	-.088	-.136	.100
Social worker	-.076	-.138	-.088	-.011	-.082	.031	-.095	-.096	-.118	-.065

*$N = 158$.

Table 13. Correlations between Theoretical Orientation Factors and Professional Activity Interests*

	Factor									
Activity	1	2	3	4	5	6	7	8	I	II
Teaching	-.005	-.076	-.063	-.069	-.038	.060	-.015	-.028	-.067	-.056
Research	.071	.142	.213	.104	.039	.040	.208	.269	.243	.000
Writing	-.226	-.091	-.170	-.123	.071	-.032	-.114	.097	-.107	.059
Administration	.014	.094	.025	.004	.158	.037	-.022	.052	.044	.072
Counseling-therapy	-.167	-.248	-.303	-.107	-.086	.092	-.248	-.221	-.299	-.102
Consulting	.065	-.079	.005	-.036	-.080	.184	.066	.012	-.012	-.151

*$N = 158$.

Table 14. Correlations between Theoretical Orientation Factors and Recreational Interests*

Activity	Factor									
	1	2	3	4	5	6	7	8	I	II
Active recreation	.089	.035	.105	.074	-.150	.100	.131	-.072	.072	-.144
Chess	.139	.067	.187	.136	.033	.173	.196	.085	.172	-.079
Card games	.157	.137	.176	.128	-.081	.052	.128	-.013	.148	-.076
Listening to music	.021	-.080	-.026	.009	-.110	.067	-.019	-.036	-.044	-.102
Dancing	-.011	-.110	-.128	-.129	-.035	-.004	-.132	-.272	-.196	-.018
Conversing	-.107	-.011	-.139	-.084	.023	-.033	-.048	-.060	-.086	.032
Drawing	-.090	-.162	-.093	-.185	-.010	.003	-.174	-.201	-.213	-.007
Watching sports	.116	.034	.058	.011	-.196	.128	.061	-.121	.015	-.187
Play or movie	-.031	-.033	-.050	-.089	.071	-.187	-.060	-.183	-.103	.147
Large party	-.022	.010	.013	.003	-.062	.102	.022	-.079	-.006	-.094
Art gallery	-.057	-.068	-.043	-.139	-.050	.010	-.016	-.046	-.079	-.035
Singing, playing music	-.081	-.176	-.262	-.144	-.020	-.124	-.178	-.141	-.239	.058
Reading novels	.058	.070	.094	-.002	-.050	-.017	.097	-.056	.059	-.019
Poetry	-.104	-.079	-.127	-.084	-.036	-.145	-.112	-.069	-.124	.062
Science fiction	-.039	.052	.045	-.082	.066	-.147	-.094	.022	-.009	.122
Nonfiction	-.069	-.071	.024	-.162	-.066	.040	-.044	-.003	-.065	-.061

*N = 158.

Table 15. Correlations between Theoretical Orientation Factors and Study of Values Scales*

Value	Factor									
	1	2	3	4	5	6	7	8	I	II
Theoretical	.004	.438	.352	.106	.118	-.102	.292	.394	.452	.127
Economic	.073	.169	.276	.117	-.042	.166	.230	.079	.244	-.122
Aesthetic	-.355	-.203	-.261	-.170	.142	-.236	-.280	-.203	-.308	.220
Social	.007	-.221	-.105	-.053	-.157	.099	-.215	-.121	-.204	-.148
Political	.016	.245	.036	.051	-.054	-.102	.042	.064	.135	.030
Religious	.255	-.260	-.198	.010	-.022	.157	-.013	-.099	-.174	-.106

*$N = 99$.

Table 16. Correlations between Theoretical Orientation Factors and Interpersonal Values*

Value	Factor									
	1	2	3	4	5	6	7	8	I	II
Support	-.066	-.085	-.191	-.086	.027	-.130	-.099	-.136	-.155	.089
Conformity	.035	-.031	.062	.031	-.023	.056	.042	.037	.033	-.045
Recognition	.070	.033	-.015	.067	.143	-.107	-.057	-.017	.003	.144
Independence	-.063	.084	.056	-.036	-.037	-.021	.116	.022	.069	-.010
Benevolence	-.110	-.305	-.133	-.195	-.145	.079	-.154	-.038	-.225	-.129
Leadership	.151	.301	.185	.180	.070	.102	.161	.121	.256	-.017

*$N = 158$.

Table 17. Correlations between Theoretical Orientation Factors and General Beliefs Factors*

General Beliefs factor	Factor								I	II
	1	2	3	4	5	6	7	8		
Theistic religion	.352	-.245	-.055	.075	-.014	.057	.128	-.011	-.053	-.042
Future-productive orientation	.039	.141	.169	.184	.102	.017	.140	.187	.225	.047
Detachment	.177	.181	.239	.098	.328	-.107	.211	.079	.227	.248
Relativism	.166	-.026	-.085	-.169	-.171	-.056	-.185	-.228	-.178	-.062
Scientism-determinism	.108	.716	.498	.352	-.074	.192	.475	.342	.681	-.156
Optimism	.078	.023	.186	.114	-.034	.197	.181	.107	.161	-.137

*$N = 99$.

Table 18. Correlations between Theoretical Orientation Survey and Psycho-Epistemological Profile*

PEP variable	Factor									
	1	2	3	4	5	6	7	8	I	II
Rationalism	.003	.057	-.047	.170	.018	.214	.083	.219	.124	-.118
Metaphorism	-.260	-.347	-.596	-.221	.149	-.133	-.475	-.123	-.494	.163
Empiricism	.260	.208	.174	.235	.089	.132	.276	.358	.339	-.029

*$N = 99$.

Table 19. Correlations between Theoretical Orientation Factors and Experience Inventory Factors*

Experience factor	Factor									
	1	2	3	4	5	6	7	8	I	II
Aesthetic sensitivity	-.099	-.176	-.217	-.224	.023	-.123	-.255	.043	-.221	.083
Unusual perceptions and associations	-.026	.059	-.259	-.231	-.001	-.064	-.127	-.012	-.139	.036
Theoretical and hypothetical ideas	-.142	.075	-.265	-.290	.003	.062	-.079	.125	-.100	-.034
Use of fantasy and dreams	.006	-.072	-.287	-.204	.067	-.069	-.138	-.041	-.196	.078
Unconventional views of reality	.018	-.315	-.295	-.091	-.170	.136	-.286	-.095	-.303	-.176
Indulgence in fantasy	-.070	.131	-.193	-.134	.107	-.103	-.127	-.003	-.072	.121
Deliberate thought	.009	.046	-.158	-.112	-.071	.108	-.003	.113	-.024	-.103

*$N = 106$.

Table 20. Correlations between Theoretical Orientation Factors and Factors of Experienced Control*

Control factor	Factor									
	1	2	3	4	5	6	7	8	I	II
1. Conscientious effort	-.145	.141	.052	-.038	-.164	.315	.158	.117	.118	-.277
2. Personal confidence	.020	.148	.226	.258	-.107	.301	.135	.286	.272	-.236
3. Capacity of mankind	.006	.406	.303	.174	-.126	.104	.284	.259	.384	-.132
4. Planning-organization	.024	.026	.006	-.014	-.054	.109	.046	-.044	.007	-.094
5. Internal processes	.094	-.056	.106	.082	-.071	.161	.108	-.039	.044	-.135
6. Social-political events	-.032	.010	-.090	-.162	-.092	.081	-.014	-.046	-.073	-.100
7. Social interaction	-.051	.147	.017	.008	.014	-.039	-.054	-.038	.031	.301

*N = 90.

Table 21. Correlations between Theoretical Orientation Factors and Myers-Briggs Variables

Myers-Briggs scale	Factor									
	1	2	3	4	5	6	7	8	I	II
Males (N = 61):										
EI	.011	.098	.078	.160	.215	−.276	.038	−.044	.092	.280
SN	−.584	−.047	−.269	−.139	.032	−.075	−.184	.127	−.138	.060
TF	.001	−.307	−.315	−.121	.105	−.158	−.213	−.123	−.302	.150
JP	−.210	−.013	−.224	−.031	.162	−.045	.001	.126	−.043	.123
Females (N = 43):										
EI	.102	.155	.167	−.068	.223	−.314	.172	.025	.147	.308
SN	−.015	.059	−.267	−.185	−.092	.076	−.069	.048	−.108	−.096
TF	−.114	−.178	−.252	−.091	−.340	.296	−.208	−.232	−.304	−.361
JP	.015	−.109	−.087	−.333	−.090	.059	−.081	−.437	−.323	−.084
Total group (N = 104):										
EI	.047	.047	.077	.014	.199	−.294	.036	−.073	.028	.282
SN	−.347	−.061	−.287	−.191	−.027	−.015	−.177	.039	−.177	−.007
TF*	−.049	−.288	−.307	−.144	−.078	.037	−.234	−.201	−.328	−.066
JP	−.118	−.071	−.184	−.144	.058	−.003	−.045	−.129	−.156	.036

*Strictly speaking, the male and female data should not be combined for the TF scale, since there are differences in the scoring of the T and F components for men and women. Despite a bit of confounding, however, the correlations for TF provide a useful picture of trends for the total group.

Table 22. Correlations between Theoretical Orientation Factors and 16PF Factors*

16PF factor	Factor									
	1	2	3	4	5	6	7	8	I	II
A. Affectothymia	-.074	-.061	-.154	-.080	.033	.067	-.201	-.305	-.204	-.019
B. Intelligence	.111	-.027	-.036	.007	.026	-.175	-.144	.080	-.031	.117
C. Ego strength	.025	-.022	.014	-.042	-.040	.156	.034	-.256	-.071	-.113
E. Dominance	-.055	.121	.017	.033	-.081	-.012	.057	-.125	.033	-.040
F. Surgency	.011	.017	.067	-.065	-.077	-.035	-.029	-.177	-.045	-.025
G. Superego strength	.038	.069	-.058	.104	.119	.131	-.026	.111	.054	-.006
H. Parmia	-.106	.036	-.054	-.106	.008	.034	-.083	-.085	-.069	-.015
I. Premsia	-.176	-.284	-.269	-.187	.048	-.297	-.347	-.149	-.326	.200
L. Protension	.024	-.018	-.071	-.112	-.077	-.096	-.071	-.018	-.072	.011
M. Autia	.044	.268	.138	.065	.101	-.038	.197	.029	.192	.081
N. Shrewdness	.077	-.046	.025	.072	-.056	.111	.066	-.045	.013	-.097
O. Guilt proneness	-.038	.143	.122	.042	-.140	.046	.088	.107	.135	-.108
Q1. Radicalism	.020	.267	.242	.113	.059	.051	.225	.256	.294	.005
Q2. Self-sufficiency	.137	.062	.003	.033	.130	-.178	-.010	.150	.064	.179
Q3. Self-sentiment control	.003	-.053	-.011	.046	.046	.189	.089	.039	.023	-.082
Q4. Ergic tension	-.260	-.061	-.097	-.106	.022	-.062	-.070	.026	-.080	.049

*N = 90.

Table A. Means and Standard Deviations on TOS Scales for 866 APA Members

Factor	32-item inventory		63-item inventory	
	Mean	SD	Mean	SD
1	9.15	3.00	18.78	5.14
2	11.67	4.01	22.74	6.88
3	10.30	3.36	19.91	5.75
4	9.94	2.87	21.04	4.96
5	11.11	3.39	23.21	5.82
6	11.82	3.75	25.45	5.72
7	10.11	3.14	17.96	5.26
8	10.59	3.20	21.48	5.47
I	52.61	11.35	103.14	20.80
II	49.29	6.11	47.76	9.92

Table B. Means and Standard Deviations on TOS Scales for 510 Male APA Members

Factor	32-item inventory		63-item inventory	
	Mean	SD	Mean	SD
1	9.34	3.22	19.10	5.48
2	12.26	4.22	23.78	7.20
3	10.50	3.56	20.33	6.19
4	10.16	2.96	21.37	5.17
5	10.93	3.37	23.05	5.93
6	11.95	3.89	25.82	5.78
7	10.49	3.38	18.56	5.69
8	10.85	3.28	22.10	5.60
I	54.25	11.94	106.14	21.95
II	48.98	6.24	47.23	10.14

Table C. Means and Standard Deviations on TOS Scales for 356 Female APA Members

| Factor | 32-item inventory | | 63-item inventory | |
	Mean	SD	Mean	SD
1	8.88	2.64	18.32	4.57
2	10.83	3.52	21.26	6.10
3	10.02	3.04	19.31	5.01
4	9.62	2.71	20.58	4.62
5	11.38	3.41	23.45	5.68
6	11.65	3.56	24.92	5.59
7	9.56	2.68	17.08	4.45
8	10.22	3.04	20.60	5.16
I	50.27	10.00	98.83	18.21
II	49.73	5.88	48.53	9.55

Index

Index